PSYCHE OF THE INJURED ATHLETE:

THE UNSPOKEN TRUTHS

DR. LAURA MIELE, PHD
2020

Psyche of the Injured Athlete
The Unspoken Truths

by Laura Miele, PhD

Copyright © 2021 Laura Miele

Published by SkillBites LLC
www.skillbites.net

All rights reserved.

For bulk orders, contact SkillBites at info@skillbites.net or 610-783-4519.

DISCLAIMER AND/OR LEGAL NOTICES

ISBN-13: 978-1-952281-38-9 paperback
ISBN-13: 978-1-952281-39-6 eBook

TESTIMONIALS

I so wish I could have had this resource when I played. As a former athlete who went through an injury early on in my career, I can reiterate to anyone that the psychology of the injury was far greater than the physical limitations. Although I truly believe my coaches and teammates and trainers had great intentions, what I experienced was deeply personal and life-changing, and the "if only I had help with my mental side" kept creeping in. Dr. Miele will change the game of sports, as she brings awareness to the psyche of elite athletes. This is a fantastic resource: a wellspring of knowledge, research, and wisdom. A must read for any coach, physical trainer, or athlete!

Tiffany Kasdorf
Softball pitcher, Florida State University ('05-'08)

As a former professional soccer player, injuries were key contributors to my never reaching the levels I knew I was capable of .... The psychological implications of what athletes go through must be better understood by not only the athletes themselves but also coaches, athletic trainers, family members, and teammates. In this book, Dr. Miele highlights the key psychological aspects that should be taken into consideration when athletes become injured. This book would have greatly assisted me in dealing with my injuries much better—so I hope it can assist anyone reading it to deal with injury and come back psychologically stronger.

Dr. Ashley Allanson, Ph.D.

Assistant Professor of Instruction in Coaching Education, Ohio University.

Professional soccer player, Hull City Tigers AFC (2003-05) and Scunthorpe United AFC (2005-07).

Dr Laura Miele really hit the nail on the head. It was so relevant to me as a former athlete and now as a coach dealing with so many young injured players. Miele has provided an outstanding book to guide coaches, athletic trainers, parents, and even athletes on the complex reality of a career-ending injury. Her firsthand account as well as those from other athletes provides an opportunity for injured athletes to learn "it's okay not to be okay." She then provides us with the "Injured Athlete Questionnaire," which should be posted in every training room, coach's office, and locker room as a great conversation starter for athletes.

Diane "Dee" Stephan

Avon, CT

CT Chapter US Lacrosse Hall of Fame 2010

Current NCAA Division III lacrosse coach at Eastern Connecticut State University

Owner and operator, coach of Dodgers Lacrosse.

Dr. Laura Miele successfully weaves her lifelong experience as an athlete, a coach, and a scholar into this relevant, relatable, and, most importantly—actionable text. This is a book you'll come back to with your highlighter!

Patricia Steen

USAT Certified Coach & 7 Time Ironman

Dr. Laura Miele has written a compelling book that is a must-read for those working with athletes dealing with season- or career-ending injuries. The personal stories (including Dr. Miele's) and professional insights are extremely helpful in understanding the psychological elements of dealing with an athletic injury.

Dr. Michael Sachs, PhD, CMPC

Professor of Emeritus, Temple University, Author and past president of the Association for Applied Sport Psychology.

I highly recommend Dr. Miele's book *Psyche of the Injured Athlete*. Having been an athlete, a sports commentator, and a coach, I found her book insightful and beneficial for athletes, coaches, parents, and others. Most athletes lose something once their athletic life comes to an end, and the transition can be particularly difficult for those whose athletic careers end due to injury. The more we share our experiences, the more we benefit and serve others who may be going through a difficult time. Dr. Miele's book not only provides numerous stories of injured athletes, it also provides proactive steps that will assist injured athletes to make the transition. All athletes and coaches can benefit from reading Dr. Miele's book.

David Diaz-Infante
2x Super Bowl Champion
NFL Coach

TABLE OF CONTENTS

ACKNOWLEDGEMENTS

Vincent Cannizzaro, Bobby Hurley, Maura McHugh, John Mishock, Tony Paolillo, Allen Watson, Jack Ryan, Samantha, McKay, Karen Self, and Tarence Wheeler. Thank you all for speaking with me and assisting in the completion of this book.

This book is dedicated to:

Mom and Dad: Thank you for your relentless love and support.

Maddison and Taylor: Always reach for the stars and know your worth.

Vanessa: Thank you for your candor and always believing in me.

David: Thank you for getting me!

Dr. Denise Autret: Thank you for being the friend that could always pull me out of my emotional rabbit hole.

Conrad McRae: Sleep in peace my friend. I know that you are winning every dunking contest up there.

Eddie Urbano: I hope you are wrestling in heaven.

Dr. Daniel Landers: Thank you for inspiring me and guiding me toward the field of Sport Psychology.

Donna Landers: I know you are smiling down from heaven as I pursue all the things you encouraged me to achieve.

My childhood girlfriends: May we continue to always silently fix each other's crowns.

My former coaches, ballers and friends who stood by me and had my back even after I was injured: Thank you for the inspiration to keep going.

The "injured" athletes: Your athletic career (at every level) has provided you with the tools necessary to guide your soul and provide you with the mental strength to be the best in every facet of your life; never give up!

FOREWORD

I cannot remember ever not having a basketball in my hand while I was growing up. My innate love for the game was almost immediate with my father at the helm of St. Anthony's men's basketball in Jersey City, New Jersey.

In my rookie year playing in the NBA, I was in a terrible auto accident. After the accident, the immense pain, fighting for my life, and realizing the impact it would have on my ability to play basketball sent me to a dark place. I was left with a huge emotional void from not being able to fulfill my career dreams and aspirations as a pro basketball player. Through the years, the emotional turbulence of the pain has surfaced in many different ways and at various times. I call them my demons. Something as simple as getting back into a car has become difficult.

When Laura approached me to be interviewed and then later asked me to write the foreword for this book, I was very interested. I appreciated that this book could assist athletes who have similarly suffered career-ending injuries. The insights provided here will also assist coaches like myself to recognize when an injured athlete is struggling so they may be able to provide the much needed support.

I have been very fortunate because of my supportive, loving family as well as the unbelievable support I received from friends and former coaches, which has enabled me not only to survive but also to learn and grow from my accident. As an NBA player, I also had the best medical attention I could get.

For those less fortunate, those who may not have access to quality medical treatment or supportive family, friends, and coaches, this book could be a lifesaver. Laura's detailed treatment of the mental side of the recovery process immediately resonated with me. Back when I played, I did not speak much about what I went through. The information in the book is more valuable today than it ever has been, as athletes' identities have become more ingrained in their sports than ever before.

Understanding how the grieving process after losing one's career aspirations works into the mindset of a former athlete is incredibly valuable, and I would recommend any injured athlete as well as anyone who participates in the development of athletes to read this book in order to properly facilitate growth after a tragic injury. I appreciate Laura involving me in such an important endeavor. The healing process for athletes after an injury—for that matter, for anyone who has suffered a major injury—is an evolving conceptual undertaking that should not be overlooked as people transition from one phase of physical and mental recovery to the next.

Bobby Hurley, Jr.
Head Men's Basketball Coach, Arizona State
First team All-America, Duke University
Former NBA player
Three-time Final Four appearance and two back-to-back national championships in 1991 and 1992
All-time leader in assists in NCAA basketball
Seventh overall first round draft pick

LETTING GO AND MOVING ON

All your life you have had a dream,
This inner fire—
This inner scheme.
You've met its success halfway,
But you run into a few obstacles
Along the way.
At times, the winds have been shades of green,
But you kept your head up and followed your dream.
You wouldn't let others get in your way.
Nothing could let that dream go astray.
You've shed many tears,
There's been a lot of pain.
Now, that inner fire has become a burning flame.
The winds have become faster
And you're trying to hold on—
Because you know you're a fighter
And you've got to stay strong.
Sometimes being strong means letting go—
Even if your heart tells you no.

Miele, 11/16/91

INTRODUCTION

This book attempts to create an intimate view of what an athlete experiences after suffering a debilitating, career-ending injury. The information provided in this book will bring light to the often-unspoken feelings of athletes on this inexplicable emotional journey. Although it speaks specifically to athletes, this book may hit home for many people who have suffered the loss of a career.

Loss tends to manifest itself in many negative ways, most notably at the start of the experience. Fortunately, the very perseverance and resilience that enables an athlete to compete at an elite level can also help them overcome the mental and physical challenges they face as a result of their injury.

My intention for this book is to help coaches, parents, medical practitioners, and the injured athletes themselves to understand what goes on in the mind of the "injured" or "broken." My hope is to provide insight into what athletes experience and how coaches and sport medicine practitioners can identify when these athletes are in emotional turmoil. Better analysis and treatment can be made to help ease the load in the journey of "injured athletes" with the hope that the healing and rehabilitation process can be expedited and made easier on the mind and heart. The lack of mental health resources since I began writing this book in 1992 still amazes me. Only now are we as a society slowly embracing the education and resources necessary to assist athletes with their rollercoaster of emotions and desire for mental well-being.

We all have our own stories to tell; while some athletes are perfectly fine transitioning out of sport, others are not. In this book, I am referring to those who are struggling with the loss of all they have worked toward.

For most athletes, their first love is for their sport. They spend every waking moment doing what they love. As athletes continue to evolve within their sport, they develop a social role that later turns into an identity. They sacrifice time with family and friends to gain more knowledge of the sport that has become their passion. It could be on the field, court, or pool, but the genesis of becoming an elite athlete encompasses every thread within a person's body. The desire to compete is something that is instilled within the athlete; it is something that is sparked by a need to be successful and the very best at their sport. They will fight through the pain just to play. Self-worth is not justified by how much better one athlete is over another, but by being a competitor and knowing what it takes to be successful.

True athletes eat, sleep, and live their sport. Sadly, they sometimes fall short. A shortcoming can often be psychologically and socially detrimental, whether it is caused by an injury, being let go by a team, or retirement. There seems to be nothing that can prepare an athlete for a career-ending injury or forced retirement from their sport. What happens when it all ends abruptly? The depression and grief that surrounds athletes can be overwhelming. Only in recent years have athletes started to speak up about their mental health issues caused by the end of their careers.

Something within our fiber as athletes prepares us for the ups and downs of life, but it may take support from others to get us through the pain of losing our athletic identities.

Although it can get buried deep within one's psyche, the inherent tenacity within the athlete to strive to be the best never goes away. Instead, it just comes back in other forms. The personification of success does not always happen in athletic competition; it can sometimes happen afterward with the tools that athletic life has provided.

As athletes, we have been taught to mask our pain and fight through it. I believe that even with the highest pain tolerance, an athlete who has suffered a career-ending injury feels pain like never before; it is akin to the loss of a loved one. Athletes are subject to mental health issues like anyone else. The only difference is that most elite athletes have worked their whole lives to become successful and earn that status. The fact that they so vehemently identify themselves by their athletic roles is a game changer when the end of those careers comes about abruptly. The coping techniques used in stressful moments of competition are gone, and their world shatters. It is amazing how quickly they lose themselves and forget what sports have taught them.

The journey of the injured athlete has been my journey, but I know it has not been mine alone. I believe that telling my story, which includes my taste of success, mental abuse, and overcoming a serious injury, will allow others to realize that they are not alone in their struggles.

We, as an athletic community, need to do better and provide our injured teammates with more assistance to help put them on the right path to recover both physically and mentally.

Evan was a basketball player. He was a sophomore in high school when he suffered a serious back injury that required surgery. After the surgery, Evan silently suffered. His mother, in an interview on the website *Sidelined*, said that she did not interpret his personality changes as a sign of depression or indication of suicidal tendencies. Evan could not handle the pain and the loss of not being able to play again and took his own life. He was only sixteen.[1]

Evan's type of suffering is not limited to teenagers, who may lack maturity or coping skills. These emotions are, in fact, very real and affect people of all ages and sports.

Former NFL player George Koonce attempted suicide in 2003. Looking back, he says: "I was in a bad place. I was fortunate enough to play football from the age of nine to thirty-two, but when the lights cut out for me, personally, in the stadium, that was tough to take. I was drinking a lot and spending time alone. I was isolated and didn't have anyone I could talk to about the issues that I was dealing with."[2]

1.   Sue Rosenstock, "Depression and the Sidelined Athlete," *Sidelined*, 2018, accessed Dec 22, 2020, https://www.sidelinedusa.org/sidelineinterviews/.

2.   Fox 6 Now Milwaukee, "Former Packers' Linebacker George Koonce on Giving Back," *Fox 6 Milwaukee*, June 11, 2012, accessed Dec 22, 2020, https://www.fox6now.com/sports/former-packers-linebacker-george-koonce-on-giving-back/.

Sometimes the loss can be too overwhelming. When Troy Vincent, former NFL vice president of player engagement and former Pro Bowl cornerback, was asked about life after the NFL, he stated, "You're talking about an identity crisis. Every athlete has to face the same question when they're done: 'Who am I?'"[3]

At times when we think that athletes are on top of the world, we are completely unaware of what they are dealing with in their private lives. Take, for instance, twenty-eight-time Olympic medal winner Michael Phelps. He has discussed his bouts of major depression that he typically experienced after the Olympics. He has confessed to using drugs and self-medicating to help him escape his depression. In 2012, Phelps decided he was not only done with his sport but done with living too. He fell into a deep depression and knew that he needed help.[4]

One point I need to get across is that when athletes lose their sport, they need time to grieve. Just like encountering a death, grieving takes time. We have to allow athletes to accept their situations in their own time, in a productive and safe manner. With that said, it is important to understand that there are identifiable signs of distress that athletes experience.

People are all affected by loss differently. Some will exhibit many different signs such as anger, frustration, or lashing out

---

3.   Jeffri Chadiha, "Life After NFL a Struggle for Many," ESPN, May 31, 2012, accessed Dec 22, 2020, https://www.espn.com/nfl/story/_/id/7983790/life-nfl-struggle-many-former-players/.

4.   Susan Scutti, "Michael Phelps: 'I Am Extremely Thankful That I Did Not Take My Life,'" CNN, January 20, 2018, accessed Dec 22, 2020, https://www.cnn.com/2018/01/19/health/michael-phelps-depression/index.html/.

for no reason, while some will retreat within themselves and tell no one of their pain. We never truly know how dark a person's mind can become. It is vitally important to reconnect the mind-body component as it is the mind that tells the body to move forward.

CHAPTER ONE

MY STORY

"To me, there is no better place to be than on a court with a basketball in my hand. To explain this is very difficult. It has been a passion and a dream. Now, there is still passion and just a different dream..." (Miele, 1992).

For me? Playing basketball was such a euphoric feeling; it fueled my inner fire. It took me to my happy place; no one could stop me or my desire to be the best. When it abruptly ended, I felt lost and alone. Who was I if I could not play ball?

As a young girl growing up in New York City, I always loved sports. Although I was very athletic, many of the other players at my grade school were still better than me. Through ambition and determination to be the best at something, I began to come into my own at the age of twelve. That "something" was eventually narrowed down to basketball, which was always my first love.

Growing up in New York, I was a huge Knicks fan. Chris Mullins was playing for St. John's and Patrick Ewing was dominating the competition at Georgetown University. At the time, Nancy Lieberman, who also grew up in New York, was the best female player ever, and I wanted to be like her. In 1984, I was glued to the television watching the summer Olympics and was fascinated by basketball player Cheryl Miller. This is when I began to realize that I could work hard and play basketball like these two women. I then began to dream of the player I wanted to become. Early on, I had this inner fire and tenacity that still burns inside me today; you either have it or you don't, and I had it.

I begged my parents to allow me to go to a sleepaway basketball camp the summer before eighth grade; it was the Poconos Invitational Basketball Camp. During eighth grade, I dominated the CYO league. As a result of my game improving so much, I had an important decision to make as to which high school to attend. Back then, Christ the King Regional High School (CK) was a powerhouse in women's basketball, but I never thought I was good enough to go there. While many of the girls who played there had been invited by the school, I was not. A priest from my parish advised me to go to school there if I had any interest in playing basketball at a higher level. Going to CK was the best decision that I ever made; it was a privilege to play among these incredible ladies.

When I tried out for the team, I was scared that I would not make it; I put my fears aside and made junior varsity. I was so excited to be part of such a huge basketball family. Margaret McKeon and Jill Cook were two All-American seniors who I looked up to, so much so that I would even try to emulate their playstyles.

One day during my freshman year, I was shooting around before practice when the athletic director (AD) came up to me and mentioned that I had a nice shot. He told me that I could be like Margaret McKeon and get a college scholarship if I kept practicing. I idolized Margaret, but it was news to me that girls could get sports scholarships. That was all the motivation I needed. I played my JV year, but I was not the best; there were a few freshmen and sophomores who were better. I was a bit discouraged by this but refused to stop practicing. I would even practice on snowy days in my backyard. It would be icy and cold, but I did not care. I was determined to get a scholarship and one day play in the Olympics.

The following year, I went back to the Poconos Invitational Basketball Camp. We would get a lot of free time to practice at the camp. Robert Kennedy, one of the owners of the camp, approached me and said that he thought I was extremely aggressive and a good defensive player, that I had a future in basketball. My coach for the week, Mario Fournier, saw the same talents in me, took me under his wing, and helped me work on my shot and the mental aspects of the game. He believed in me even more than I believed in my-self. He told me that I needed to play ball with the boys if I wanted to improve. I was more determined than ever.

Once I returned home from camp, off I went. Hoffman Park was right down the road from my house.

I began playing and earning respect from the guys who played there. I played at the park every summer until I grad-uated high school. I was even invited to play on the City League for Boys in 1987. I got to play pick-up games with some friends like Kenny Anderson (Georgia Tech/NBA) and Conrad McRae (Syracuse). It was the best experience ever; I knew that my dream of participating in the 1992 Olympics was getting closer to becoming a reality.

During the next season, I was moved up to Varsity at the end of my sophomore year to play in the state championship series. My teammates were less than welcoming. I believe that on any team, there is a fear of losing your "spot," and I guess I posed a threat. Unsurprisingly, most of the girls who did not play much turned their backs and stopped talking to me. Since my high school was a powerhouse of basketball players, many girls from my school had come there to play and to be noticed as a dominant player. The competition was fierce; our bench was ten girls deep with pure basketball tal-ent even with five players on the court, and that is not an exaggeration.

I was not that kind of person, so I had a difficult time dealing with what I now believe to be immature and jealous teammates. I was fortunate enough to have the freshman men's basketball coach, Gerry "Ing" Ingenito, to guide me. Ing would tell me to just play and not worry about making friends because I had friends off the court. Ing helped me keep my head straight, let me know when I was screwing up, and instilled in me a great sense of confidence. He was like an older brother who was there to watch my back. That year, Christ the King girls' basketball was on the map as nationally ranked, and it had not lost a league game in years.

By my junior year of high school, I was ranked as the seventh-best basketball player in the state of New York. I became a more dominant player on the team, but the athletic director was unhappy. He was remarkably close with one of the seniors on the team (let's call her Mary). He had taken her under his wing as a freshman. I was younger by a year. However, he did the same for me as I had been his star pitcher for his varsity softball team since my freshman year. As the AD and Head Softball coach, he had his favorites; however, Mary came first, and he did not want me to play better or outshine her especially in basketball.

Looking back, this still hurts me emotionally. The reason that I mention this is so that other former athletes know that we all have been through different facets of emotional turmoil. It appears in different capacities. We can all be injured, not only due to the loss of sport but the process of being part of our sport.

During basketball season in my junior year, this AD began to take me out of my typing class two to three times each week. He would have me come down to his office and tell me that I was doing too well in the basketball games and that I was averaging too many points; it was not fair to Mary. According to him, I should not be taking away her limelight during her senior year.

I did not understand what I was doing wrong. He would curse at me, saying, "Who the fuck do you think you are?" And he used many other expletives to tear me down and break me. Despite being a priest, this man had a bad temper and a dark side to him. He told me that he would make sure that I did not receive any scholarships if I continued to score in double digits. I was mortified, scared, and confused. I turned to my good friend Carl, who told me to ignore the AD, but this was exceedingly difficult to do as I felt that he had my future in his hands. After all, he would bring me to his office, speak to me for fifteen to twenty minutes, send me back to class in tears, and no one noticed. This went on for the entire duration of my junior year basketball season.

The AD told me that if I continued to outscore Mary, he would withhold all my incoming college recruitment letters. Petrified for my future, I would not even go to my parents. If anyone knew my dad, they knew he would have gone to CK, priest or not, and had more than words with him.

When I look back at this, I realize that I suffered through some serious mental abuse. His actions hurt me down to my core. More than that, I looked up to him—the whole team thought that he hung the moon (well, most of us), and I was crushed that he would do this to me. He made me feel like a bad person. He threatened that if I ever told anyone, I would have no future in collegiate sports. I thought this man had so much power back then; I wonder now why I didn't tell my parents or anyone else. This bothers me as I think of other athletes who have suffered similar abuse, even physical abuse, at the hands of a coach or superior figure in a school or athletic arena. We feared the ramifications of reporting what happened to us. I look back and wish I had stepped up, but I was so worried that all of my hard work would be for nothing because of this man. In hindsight, I should have reported him. I gave him too much power. I do not recommend ever keeping something like this to yourself.

The great part of playing for CK was that every year we would play schools from around the country. This gave us so much exposure to be recruited. My junior year, our team traveled to the University of Texas. This was a team I had dreamed of playing for, and my coach had set up two games there. He had hoped that I would impress the coaches enough that they would offer me a scholarship. I immediately fell in love with Austin, Texas.

The night before the first game, there was a knock on my door at midnight. One of my teammates said that the AD wanted me to come to his hotel room. It was midnight—why didn't a red flag go off inside me and say no! As I walked into the room, I noticed that my coach was not present, but the seniors and one freshman were. The AD then proceeded to tell me that the girls would go around and say what they needed to say to me, and I just needed to listen and stay quiet. It was one of the worst experiences of my life to that point.

The AD ridiculed me as a player and as a person off of the court. He stated that I hung out with too many black male players and he did not like that. He then said that I was overshadowing the seniors and I needed to pass the ball to them more. The crazy thing was, I was never a selfish player; I was always happy to see other girls shine. It is an ideology that I still maintain today.

Then, each of the players had their turn to say what they wanted about me, but I was not allowed to defend myself. I was devastated. In hindsight, this was his way to let me know that I had to wait my turn. He told me that the ball had to go in other players' hands and stay out of mine. I could not believe that not one of those girls stood up for me.

Not only would I never have taken part in that kind of behavior, but I would also have defended the person on the receiving end of such ridicule. Afterward, I went back to my hotel room and cried like a baby. It was the first time in my life I contemplated suicide. I did not tell any adults of the incident (only my friend Carl) out of fear that the AD would ruin my future career in basketball. All these years later, I implore everyone to teach any child to always tell— no matter what. I literally just told my parents the story in 2019. To think that I wanted to jump out of the hotel window that night; my parents would have been devastated and would never have had any answers. I was sixteen years old; I thought I had to be tough and suck it up. The one thing I finally did right was to tell a friend. Even though the abuse did not stop, I was able to see what the AD was trying to do, and I overcame the abuse. Nonetheless, I should have told an adult.

The next game, I scored only one point. The following game, I scored maybe two points. Furious, my coach took me aside at halftime and asked me why I was not shooting the ball when the University of Texas was looking to recruit me. He told me that if I did not begin shooting, he would bench me. I still said nothing. I was a frozen in fear. My coach had no idea what I had gone through the night before, and I most certainly did not tell him. All I could think of was that I was a bad person, wondering why my team would turn on me. I was lost! Vinny, my coach, had no clue what had happened to me that night.

VINNY CANNIZZARO

I am a former women's basketball coach at Christ the King Regional High School in Queens, New York. I coached Laura Miele while she played high school basketball. During my coaching career, I was not one to get too into the mental side, but back then not many coaches had the tools to assist their athletes with any type of emotional or mental issues. I think that many athletes have a hard time dealing with adversity. Adversity could come in different forms from injury, pressure to play and prove oneself, family issues, and/or academic. From a coaching standpoint, there is a rite of passage, and an athlete who can push through the adversity will be successful. It cannot always be perfect. You may wonder: "How do athletes handle adversity?" or "Do you give up or work harder?" Whatever happens, athletics has conditioned you to overcome whatever obstacle is thrown at you!

Subsequently, I questioned myself as a person and a player. I was a very fun-loving, naïve, young girl. I was tough as nails when I played on the court, but off of the court I was a mush.

I believe that all the abuse the AD put me through affected that pivotal season for me. I felt like every move I made would be scrutinized, so even though I got serious, what did it matter if the AD was up my ass? No child should ever have to feel that way. High school has enough pressure as it is.

At the end of the 1988 season (my junior year), we made it to the state championship series again. As a clutch player, I hit a thirteen-foot buzzer shot to win the semifinal that got us into the state championship. Of course, everyone seemed to love me then.

The summer of 1988, I played AAU for the New York Liberty Belles and Riverside Church. With these teams, I was taught to persevere and not take any shit. Most of all, I learned how to be a leader on the court, which was something that I had to suppress while playing for Christ the King. I began to suffer from exercise-induced asthma but forced myself to fight through it. Not being able to breathe would make me physically weak, affect my shot, and sometimes my overall game. It was during this time that I first had to experience fighting my psyche.

In hindsight, I do believe that my breathing issues were a manifestation of the anxiety and fear I had to suppress from the months of emotional abuse I was subjected to by that AD. My anxiety heightened during those times, but my asthma took its toll on me while I played. I looked and felt weak, all the while hearing that AD's voice in my head every time I played. I would question my passes, moves, and shot. It was only when I got into "the zone" that I was able to escape my thoughts.

Riverside Church was invited to play a tournament in Arizona. As soon as we explored the Arizona State University (ASU) campus, I was hooked! I wanted to be a part of the Pac-10. My dream of playing at University of Texas–Austin was gone. My father pushed for Duke, but all I wanted was to get back to Arizona. I was going to play at ASU and get to Barcelona, Spain, for the 1992 Olympics. I had big dreams for myself and my future.

The Fall of my senior year, I was ranked the number one player for New York City and State and was awarded the New York State 1989 Gatorade Player of the Year. By then, I had already received and accepted a full scholarship to play as a shooting guard for Arizona State University and started there in 1989. Unfortunately, I injured my back during my freshman year. I went through physical therapy and sat out the rest of the season. Because of the injury, I had to work with my physical therapist to relearn how to shoot, squat for defense, and pass.

Sophomore year, I was able to practice and play again, and I thought I was ready to go, even though I was still experiencing simultaneous hamstring and back pain. But soon enough, one day at practice, I froze: I could not move due to the excruciating pain. My back had gone out, and I had lost feeling in my left leg. That was the beginning of the end of my dream and my collegiate basketball career.

We were going into Pac-10 play, and my coach, Maura McHugh, had asked me to play. She told me she wanted me on the court and did not care if I practiced only one day a week. When my teammates got wind of it, I felt like I was back in high school all over again. They were not happy.

They thought: "Why should she get to play when she did not put the practice in?"

I look back and think I should have said, "Fuck all of them! This is my life, my career," but I felt it was not right. I was in a tremendous amount of physical pain, but I wanted to play so badly. I felt alone and isolated.

Recently, my cousin Vanessa and I were talking about the importance of social support. She tells her athletic sons that no matter what you go through, you should find your person. Identify with some adult at a level in which you are able to speak to them candidly in the event you really need them. Having "your person" is vital in certain circumstances. It would have been so beneficial to have a support system in place for me as an injured athlete, but these things did not exist at the time. I often think about what would have happened if I had spoken more about what I had experienced—maybe a different decision or outcome? Those are questions I will never have answers to, and as easy as it was for people to say, "get over it," for some reason I could not. Depression began to set in.

MAURA MCHUGH

I coached basketball for twenty-five years at both the Division I college level and the professional level in both the ABL and the WNBA. I am considered somewhat of a pioneer of women's basketball, because during my college career at Old Dominion University, I and four of my teammates were awarded the nation's first ever women's basketball scholarships. Although I enjoyed coaching basketball, nothing compared to playing. That is why I have a great deal of empathy for athletes who sustain career-ending injuries.

While coaching at Arizona State, I recruited Laura from Christ the King High School in NY. I was familiar with Christ the King not only because it was one of the top high school programs in the country but also because I had recruited other players from that school. Their coach, Vincent Cannizzaro, was a good mentor and was known for preparing players for the next level. The thing that really stood out for me about Laura was her mental and physical toughness and competitiveness on the court. She was a big guard that possessed excellent skills and athleticism. She was the perfect fit for my coaching style and the Pac 10 Conference.

When practice started Laura's freshman year, she proved to be just the player I had envisioned. But shortly thereafter, Laura started to experience severe back pain. We addressed her problem with the training staff who offered the usual physical therapy treatments. When her back showed no improvement, she was referred to a team physician. It should be noted that back in the day, women's basketball was not a priority at most universities. Women's programs usually received the less experienced athletic trainers and medical staff while football and men's basketball were assigned the A teams. We also had the unfortunate luck of being assigned a doctor who was not known for his love of women's athletics. He was old school and didn't see the value in sports for women. When it was deemed necessary for Laura to have back surgery in order to compete, this doctor strongly discouraged surgery claiming that she could end up in a wheelchair and might not be able to have children. I was absolutely flabbergasted. Of course, all surgery has its risks, but I knew that numerous male athletes at the university had had back surgery and were not given such dire and unrealistic prognoses. Not willing to accept this, I urged Laura to go outside the athletic department and get a second opinion. Unbeknownst to me, this doctor contacted Laura's parents directly and convinced them that surgery would put their daughter at great risk and that there was a chance she would never walk again. Naturally, Laura's parents were alarmed and felt that surgery was too risky, and she should quit basketball. I was angry and frustrated by this whole chain of events, but at this point, my hands were tied, and I had to respect the wishes of the family. (It should be noted that later in life, Laura did have surgery and went on to be a competitive boxer and still plays basketball to this day in a men's basketball league. Oh yeah, and she also has two beautiful children and no wheelchair!)

Athletes who experience career-ending injuries go through not only a great deal of physical pain but mental anguish as well. Their personal identities are caught up in being an athlete and losing that part of themselves is a huge blow to their psyches. As a coach, losing a key player to injury is devastating and can change the whole trajectory of a season and a program. Not only is the player going through a great loss, the coach and team experience this loss as well.

Coach McHugh wanted me to stay as part of the team and hang around practices, yet I could not travel with the team because I was injured. Little by little, I felt the loss of camaraderie. My teammates did not know what I was going through. They just saw me sitting on the sidelines thinking I was lucky because I did not have to endure the intense practices.

At one point, a teammate said to me, "I wish that I was injured so I wouldn't have to play anymore." This made me furious because I loved playing basketball more than life itself.

While sitting on the sidelines, I would fall asleep while watching practice because of the medications that I was taking. I did not want to be out there watching; it hurt too much. Coach McHugh wanted me to watch and learn, so of course, my falling asleep pissed her off. I fell into a depression and just began to stay away. In hindsight, I wish I had not; I wish I'd had the confidence to tell Coach McHugh what I wanted because I know she would have helped me. I was so messed up that I did not think that I deserved to ask her. With the doctors telling me that I would never be strong enough to maintain a pregnancy due to my injuries and warning me that I may never walk right again, I just could not think straight. Again, this is where having a support system for athletes would have been a tremendous help.

A deeper depression set in with suicidal thoughts and lots of drinking my sophomore year. It's not something I'm proud to admit, but I was 3,000 miles away from my real family and had just lost my athletic one. I conceded it was wise to only play ball recreationally and coach youth boys' basketball.

I believe that all student-athletes should be assigned some type of advocate. Student-athletes are young, inexperienced and need proper guidance with or without being injured.

After the injury, I could not believe that my career was ending, though through countless doctors' visits, not one said I should play again. My Uncle Denis had said to me, "You would see a hundred doctors if one told you that you could play again." He was right. The doctors that I saw were all male. I felt that in their eyes, they wondered what the big deal was if I could never play again at a higher level. Well, to me it was the kiss of death. It is amazing how sexist times were in the early 90s.

When I went home to New York during the summer of 1992, I sat in front of the television and cried. I cried that whole summer. My mother did not really understand my pain as she was not an athlete. She asked me, "When are you going to get over it?"; she said that I needed to let it go. Well, the truth was that I did not know how to; I was so sad and filled with grief.

During my senior year in 1993, I finally had back surgery. I was like a new person. I continued to play recreationally. In the spring of 1995, I had an opportunity to play professionally overseas in Wolfenbüttel, Germany; needless to say, it was short-lived. Since the offer to play was less than optimal and while still plagued with a back injury... I chose to pass. Another regret I have today.

During the summers that I came home from ASU, I would play ball at Hoffman Park as usual. One summer, the guys from the park were short a player and asked me to play in a Pro-Am tournament with them. We played at Rucker Park. During that game, I caught the eye of one of the coaches who then ask me to play for his team. I ended up having some awesome teammates like Jamal Faulkner and Shannon Shell. I remember playing against Lloyd Daniels, a streetball legend who had done a short stint at the University of Las Vegas. This guy would be drugged up and hitting shots from half court; it was as amazing as it was sad. Even though I could no longer play for ASU, I played whenever I could. My back would hurt, but I pushed through because I just loved to play.

In 1996, the American Basketball League was forming a women's professional league. I was invited to go try out at Emory College in Atlanta, Georgia. Out of the first 500 and something players, I made it to the top sixty.

The night before the last tryout, a former assistant coach came up to me and said, "Hey, Miele—how is that back holding up?" The next day, I was cut. I was devastated once again.

By the time the WNBA rolled around, my confidence was gone, and I did not even push to get a tryout. I still had back issues, but I believe my self-esteem from the past always haunted me. My mentor from Arizona State University, Donna Landers, convinced me to complete my master's degree so I could teach and coach. I still played as much basketball with men in pickup games as humanly possible. I just loved to play. I began teaching and coaching, but my personal life turned into one mistake after another for about fifteen years. I made countless poor choices with no foresight of collateral damages; I could not get over the loss of my basketball career and overall identity.

Finally, I settled into a new career; I had found my calling. I was able to teach physical education while coaching volleyball, basketball, and softball. I was in heaven. I bounced around from school to school until I found my happy place. Eventually, I came to Cesar Chavez High School in Laveen, Arizona. In 2001, the Women's Professional Football League had a full contact team in Arizona, and, on the night of my thirtieth birthday I ran into my very good friend Angel, who told me that she was the quarterback and that I should play too. I played tight end for two years with her on two different teams. The camaraderie was awesome. Due to a short stint with a knee injury, I chose to stop playing because I had a career and needed to function physically. For a short while, being part of a team again was just incredible.

By March of 2003, I had moved back to Queens, New York. One night, I went to go play basketball at the Lost Battalion Hall in Rego Park. I used to play ball there during the winter in high school. After playing, I went downstairs to lift weights and found a boxing area. I walked up to one of the guys who ran it and asked him how I could become a boxer. Tony Paolillo was the man who later became my trainer and a huge influence in my life. Tony spent countless hours teaching me the fundamentals of boxing, and he eventually instilled the love of the sport in me. He would provide me with fight films to review. I thought to myself: I have a chance to make it in another sport. So, Tony and I trained tirelessly Monday through Thursday nights. He told me to become a member of the USA boxing association and that I was ready to spar and train specifically for the Golden Gloves. That was in April, but in November, my back went out again. This time, I could not even walk.

Once again, another dream was taken away. I had surgery on December 26, 2003, ten years after the date of my first surgery out in Arizona. But I was in the semifinals of the Golden Gloves and had thirteen weeks to train following my extensive lower back surgery. Tony wanted me to stop and rehab and train for the next year, but I refused. We had worked so hard, and I did not want to let him and myself down. So, I trained in the pool under the direction of my friend and personal trainer, Jeff. I was doing well, but I was still very weak. I was able to get my upper body very strong, but my legs and abs were not what they used to be. Nonetheless, I fought in that semifinal. Even though I lost, I proved to myself that I could push through as I wish I had at Arizona State. Tony helped me to regain the confidence that had been stripped from me in high school.

Maybe it was not about basketball after all, and I should have put more value on taking lessons from the game and translating them into real life. Being an athlete taught me how to persevere under stressful situations, become a team player, and appreciate the values of hard work and discipline.

In hindsight, I realize it took me a long time to recover from my original injury. I lacked the social support necessary to get over the mental speed bumps I hit along the way. At the time, my confidence was drained because I could not help but feel like I was a bad person. Unfortunately, that was instilled in me during some formative years in high school, and it took me almost fifteen years to fight those mental demons. Was I weak to allow that to happen to me so many years ago? Why didn't I stand up for myself and tell someone? Why didn't I tell Coach McHugh what I really wanted? Maybe she could have helped.

Being brought up in New York, I thought I was weak if I cried about my feelings, so I internalized them all and let them fester inside me. For years, I was in a dark place. I would get this feeling in the pit of my stomach like my skin was crawling whenever I hit adverse times. I think I faced so much adversity early on as a teenager that I became lost. Then, when the only thing in my life that I worked so hard to achieve was gone, so was I.

I was such a mess back then. I struggled with who I was for years after my injury at ASU. Tony had no idea what he did for me during that time, but he absolutely saved me and my psyche. After that, I began to find myself and realize that I could fill the void left by my injury in other ways. I completed my doctorate, worked as a personal trainer, coached a myriad of sports, and eventually became a sports psychology consultant. I had researched exercise, sports safety, and sports injury for so many years that I was ready to find a career path that would allow me to do what I love in a different capacity. Don't get me wrong—I still played basketball and softball through the years, but I finally stopped sabotaging myself by choosing the wrong men, getting caught up in toxic relationships and drinking too much. Finally, I had found myself.

When I speak to many other athletes whose careers have been cut short, I find that this is not unusual. Some athletes never recover. Quality of life after the end of a sports career manifests itself in different ways for an uncertain period of time. The time it may take for one athlete may not be the time it takes for another to get back into their routine and begin a new way of life.

CHAPTER TWO

THE ROLE OF SPORT

The role that sports play in an athlete's life can shape their identity. The positive feelings of success in one's sport can cause athletes to associate and reinforce their sports with who they are as people.

When I ask former athletes to tell me about themselves, typically they begin with "Well, I am an athlete. This is the sport I do. This is who I am." Most athletes identify themselves in their athletic roles. They work hard to develop the fundamentals necessary to excel at their sports, never thinking that this role will one day come to an end. The reasons vary for why people participate: personal growth, self-worth, a sense of well-being, or the camaraderie of being on a team. All these things promote an athlete's love of sports, thus boosting an intrinsic drive to participate.

Sports are also a vehicle for student athletes to receive a free education and possibly continue to a professional career. Despite the many benefits derived from participating in sports, athletes often forget the gift that has been given to them until it is taken away. We all hear of the pro athletes who hold out for incomprehensible salaries and seem to forget what led them to strive to be the best in the first place. Yet, if one of those athletes suffers a serious injury, they will quickly remember how great they felt when they were playing and know that all the money in the world would not matter if they could just play again.

A sport itself may provide an opportunity for an athlete to work successfully with others, gain respect for others' differences, and achieve discipline and commitment. The tools provided by a sport can transcend into one's future. Regardless of whether these athletes attain success out in the streets or in an organized sport, they do it for the love of the game. While sports allow athletes to learn about others, they also provide them with experiences to better understand themselves.

Coaches will take athletes in when they recognize that a player needs more help off the court than on. When I coached, I practiced this philosophy with my players. I tried to identify struggling players and do whatever I could to assist them. For me, it was about what life lessons my athletes could learn through sports rather than what sports could give to them for a moment in time. I believe that I coached this way because I knew one day the playing would end and my athletes would need to find other outlets and passions.

Many athletes possess the motivation to get better at their sports, while other athletes who have talent do not always have the drive to improve. Regardless of the reasoning, elite athletes have an intense drive to be successful. This is something that athletes sometimes forget they have when circumstances are not optimal. Athletes develop physical tools to help their mental performance, but they have not learned exactly how to use those same tools to overcome obstacles that appear after the competition ends. This needs to change. We need to provide athletes with the necessary skill sets to prepare them for their lives without sports.

There are many types of pressures hidden within the realm of sports, the first being the pressure from family. The second pressure lies within the athletes themselves to strive to be the best no matter the cost. Finally, the third pressure comes from coaches who always expect the best output. Family pressures can be very overwhelming because parents may find themselves living vicariously through their children and expect them to be more successful than they were. This causes tremendous internal pressure and stress. The athletes will think that if they fail, then they will fail the most important people in their lives. However, the worst form of pressure stems from the athletes themselves. Most people are their own worst critics, and athletes are sometimes their own worst enemy when it comes to competition. The stress of athletes is emphasized in the want and need for success and to prove themselves to others. Herein lies the motivation.

ATHLETE PASSION AND MOTIVATION

Passion is the underlying force that fuels our strongest emotions. It can also be described as the intensity felt when people participate in a sport or activity that interests them deeply. Passion fills athletes with energy and empowers them to perform at their peaks.

Most young athletes who aspire to elite-level sports have played sports from an early age. The huge commitment, both physical and emotional, is often made at the expense of education, work, family, and other interests. Athletes often design everything else in their lives to fit their sports' schedules. They are motivated by the excitement they feel when they participate, and the attention that success brings can cause them to escape from the real world.

An interesting factor in the whole pursuit of athletic excellence lies in one's motivation. All athletes are driven for some reason or another, be it intrinsically or extrinsically. This is the source of an athlete's desire to be successful and the best at what they do. A successful athlete either had coaches who inspired them to be the best, possessed something inside of them that made them want to succeed, or had the benefit of both factors. It is a passion that drives them forward like fuel in a car. Athletes who are driven possess some form of motivation. For athletes motivated intrinsically, their rewards are being on that playing field doing what they love the most and achieving personal goals in the process. Their rewards are knowing they are successful due to their own thorough hard work and dedication.

Not all athletes have desires that are intrinsically motivated. To be intrinsically motivated, athletes are looking to accomplish a certain goal with no strings attached, no special incentive, and no reward. Some athletes participate for the extrinsic rewards, such as being recognized as part of the team, the euphoric feeling they get from playing, or their overall love of the game. Others participate to make a parent happy, to exercise, or to use athletics as a shield against a troubling childhood or abuse. It is easy to hide behind sports when there are issues at home. Many athletes use sports as a vehicle to place themselves elsewhere. This vehicle allows them to be strong in a game when they cannot control their home environment. A sports team offers a safe place for some athletes; for others, their team could be the only family they have.

All athletes who are successful are motivated in some way. Virtually all athletes have goals, and most goals are at least partially extrinsic. However, true performance and passion must come from within.

WHAT IS MOTIVATION?

Motivation can be defined as "the direction and intensity of one's effort."[5] Motivation is viewed in many different ways, and each person has their own personal view on how motivation works. It is a desire and a drive to work toward and compete at the highest level. Motivation can come from internal and external sources. It is the key variable of both learning and performing in sports.[6]

There are different theories on motivation and different reasons for an athlete's motivation. Some athletes are led by fear of failure, while others are led by achievement. Fear of failure can stem from the inappropriate use of rewards by a parent or coach or from an athlete never having experienced failure before. This motivation reminds me of an athlete whom I played with in college: Karen O'Connor-Self. Karen states, "My motivation is fueled by my deep insecurity and massive fear of failure." She was a determined basketball player and had all the tools to lead our team. However, she too suffered from a career-ending injury. Here is her story.

5.   Robert Weinberg and Daniel Gould, *Foundations of Sport and Exercise Psychology* (Champaign, IL: Human Kinetics, 1999).

6.   Weinberg and Gould, *Foundations*.

KAREN O'CONNOR-SELF

I played basketball for literally my entire life, so much so that I do not remember a time when I was not playing. Somewhere around middle school, the commitment to basketball began to feel like a chore. While I excelled at the game, the intensity and volume I was playing began to erode the joy I had found in playing. I struggled with burnout for many years but continued to find success. After an accolade filled high school career, I was blessed to receive a scholarship to play at Arizona State University. Once there, my teammates helped my find joy in the game, and as a result, I found a fair amount of success in the Pac-10. I even began to feel I had a promising future in playing professionally in Europe. Unfortunately, a severe back injury significantly limited my junior season and even cut my senior year short.

I was injured in a spring workout after my sophomore season, but my injury was not recognized as significant for several months. This led to surgery prior to my junior season. As a leader on the team and a significant contributor, I perceived tremendous pressure to come back sooner than was recommended. Instead of taking a year off as recommended, I chose to play and never really gave my body time to heal. My contribution to the team suffered and my individual stats dropped significantly that next season.

After the significant drop in my performance, I began to cycle through the stages of injury. Having no plans or career paths, I often asked myself: "Who am I without basketball?" Many times, successful athletes tend to define themselves solely by their success in their sport. My dreams vanished overnight and dealing with this loss was very challenging. For many years, I would look back and play the "what could have been" game.

My senior year, I was quite debilitated, and I could hardly play. During most of our practice days I was on the sideline cheering for teammates or shooting free throws by myself. I would play games on the weekends and try to recover throughout the week. When I finally took time off to give my body a chance to heal, it did, and I rarely felt any pain. I was eventually able to try out for a few pro teams as the WNBA came into existence. I think it is incredibly difficult to accept the end of your playing career, no matter how it comes to be. When your career ends due to injury, there is always that question that remains about how good you could have been if only you hadn't been hurt. When I fell short of making a WNBA team, it finally hit me that I was done. Knowing that I would never compete again was a terrible blow. I felt wholly inadequate. At this time, I was already finding success as a high school basketball coach in AZ. The sense of loss I felt in falling short took a huge toll on me. It wasn't until one of my players pointed out that I constantly wore flip flops to summer practices and hadn't laced up my sneakers in six months that I realized how withdrawn I was feeling from the game. In terms of playing, I was done. I always had that thought in the back of my head wondering if I had not been hurt and had played in Europe, would I have been able to play in the WNBA? It was a tough pill to swallow.

Today, I see it differently. Now, I have a great marriage, four kids, and an unbelievable coaching career. Through my experiences with a back injury, I learned many life lessons that helped me mature in major ways. Although my journey was hard, I learned that on the other side of hard, there is always growth! There will always be an athlete's mentality inside of me, and I do miss the camaraderie of being on a team. That is really the biggest take away from a life of athletics. The individual accolades really mean nothing, it is the lifelong friends that we develop that shape us as individuals. I find that as I get older, I shy away from any attention I receive for coaching successes. Some want attention for success, but I just want to fly under the radar and enjoy the fact that I am lucky enough to still be a part of a team.

The message I try to give my players throughout their career is that they are so much more than just a basketball player. I want them to know basketball ends eventually and limiting how they perceive themselves as human beings will only be selling themselves short. Before they leave to play college ball, we coaches take them out and try to explain to them what to expect from the college experience. We make sure to emphasize the importance of developing themselves as whole people and not just as athletes. When competition comes to end, they need to be able to find value in themselves outside of sport. By providing athletes with the mental tools to understand that there is another life for them outside their sports, the transition into the working world may be a bit easier.

Athletes who suffer the loss of their relationships with sports are most definitely suffering a serious loss. Both Kubler-Ross's stages of dying and stages related to coping with grief have been used to describe the athlete's response to retirement as a progression through stages related to feelings such as shock, numbness, anger, depression, understanding, and acceptance.[7]

The post-playing years can be challenging for athletes. For individuals who have spent most of their lives as athletes, entering unprepared into the real world where their athletic talents may not be useful can be very frightening. It is often difficult for them to find and hold a job. They may be forced to start at the bottom due to the lack of career options, which

---

7.   J. Crook and S. Robertson, "Transitions Out of Elite Sport," *International Journal of Sport Psychology* 22 (1991): 115–21.

leads to them experiencing anger, frustration, and loss of self-esteem.

Let us not forget that when an athlete enters the limelight, they transform in one way or another. This transformation is even worse when their career ends. There are even movies that depict the career termination of an athlete and their subsequent emotional turmoil. For a moment, let us look back on a movie that resonates with me and that displays how an athlete must not handle the end of their career. The movie *Everybody's All-American* stars Dennis Quaid. It is about a quarterback whose whole identity revolves around being an athlete—the hero and the star. When his career comes to an end, he loses himself and comes to realize how self-indulged he really is regarding his effort and sacrifice to be the best. He was always too caught up in his athleticism and fame. Ultimately, his retirement forces him to realize what is important in his life, such as his friends and family.

Many athletes develop extremely narrow identities of their self-worth that almost entirely depend on their ability and success at their sport. Injured athletes in particular are likely to experience an identity crisis. The more the athlete identifies himself or herself with their sport, the more intense the identity crisis will be.

It is common for athletes to become depressed when their careers are over, especially when the ending is abrupt. Most athletes never want the competition to end. Depression hits each athlete in a different way. Some pull away from family and friends and seclude. Others find themselves getting involved in gambling, drinking, drugs, and other counterproductive activities as they try to deal with the reality of their sports careers being over.

For instance, in the Netflix short series *Losers*, the episode regarding Jack "Blackjack" Ryan expresses how Jack went to a dark place when he was cut by the New Jersey Nets. He was so lost and overwhelmed with grief that he contemplated suicide. This is a person who had staked his identity on what he does, meaning if his career in basketball was going poorly, Ryan himself felt the same way. Then, he was picked up by the Harlem Wizards. He was able to take his love for basketball to a new level and get paid for it. At age 59, he still plays and performs doing what he loves the most.

Athletes who experience this depression need to understand that it is situational, and they should seek support from friends and family. When an athlete's career ends involuntarily, there is a greater chance that there will be a negative emotional and social adjustment. Therefore, the more social support, the better for the athlete's recovery. If they feel they are alone, then it can be a downward spiral into a very dark place.

ALLEN WATSON

I was a great all-around athlete growing up, so much so that I became a Division I pitcher in baseball. When I was in college, I was picked up by the St. Louis Cardinals' minor league team, and from there I went to play for the Seattle Mariners, New York Mets, and the Yankees.

I pitched at my very best when I played for the Yankees. Unfortunately, a shoulder injury and subsequent neck injury made it so I could never pitch again, which devastated me. It hurt because it was all I did all in my life. After that, I began drinking every day and fell into a major depression because my whole life was centered around baseball. I never thought I would have another job, so my career-ending injury truly hit me hard.

I was fortunate enough to have social support from my family and friends. Losing the camaraderie, I had with my teammates was one of the more difficult obstacles I had to overcome. Without baseball, I started to participate in negative behaviors such as gambling just to feel part of some competition. I was going down a bad path, but the support I received from my wife and children helped me see that there were other ways to deal with this loss.

CHAPTER THREE

THE PSYCHE OF THE INJURED ATHLETE

Psyche can be characterized as the mind's deepest thoughts or feelings. When an athlete experiences injury, their psyche becomes "injured" mentally, spiritually, and/ or emotionally. An injury for any athlete can be a very difficult experience. Their emotional state following an injury can increase stress levels depending on the way the athlete perceives what the injury entails. A severe injury can cause a surge of emotions to transpire along with the fear. Subsequently, the athlete poses the question: Is my career over?

The loss of a sports career, no matter the type of sport or how early or late in a career, still feels as if the carpet was pulled right out from under your feet without warning, like hitting a brick wall. It takes time and strength to remember the past and let go. This is not always an easy task for someone who was on their way to a potential plush career in the athletic domain.

Athletes begin to question their perception of themselves and how others perceive them. Some begin to wonder whether they quit too soon and question why this happened to them and whether they will ever find life worth living without sports.

Not only is their career lost, but the friendships and the camaraderie that was built gets lost too. When you are on a team, you have a family of people with whom you share the same lifestyle and mentality, but that family is lost once you become injured because you are no longer on the same track as your teammates. The life of the team continues on without you. So, now the athlete suffers two losses: first their career, and second, their team.

When something so personal that you have sacrificed so much for is taken away, it is a loss like no other. It is a death or divorce from a part of one's self. A part has died, and it leaves a void that you spend the rest of your life trying to fill. This discussion does not only refer to athletes. There are many people who identify so strongly with their careers that they are affected greatly if said career should end abruptly.

As with a death, there may never be a full acceptance of the loss of one's career. Some athletes may be satisfied with their careers, but the constant struggle to be the best will still exist within many former injured athletes.

Once the partial acceptance is made, then comes the motivation to pick one's bottom off the floor and do something else, much as Bobby Hurley Jr. described when he retired. He dabbled in horse racing and other business ventures, but he was not fulfilled and found his way back to the game as a coach. The haunting thoughts of his accident (which he called his "demons") and the loss of his basketball career must have been excruciating for him, yet when I spoke to him, he seemed so calm about it.

BOBBY HURLEY JR.

I came from a family where basketball was everything. My father, Bobby Hurley Sr., was the head coach for the powerhouse St. Anthony's High School in Jersey City. I had an innate love for the game of basketball. I was lucky enough to attend practices and watch my father coach. Whenever I was out playing basketball, my self-esteem could change depending on the game.

I played for my father in high school and received a full ride to play for Coach K. at Duke, a Division I university. From there, I was drafted by the Sacramento Kings. During my rookie season in 1993, I was driving home from a game at the Arco Arena when I was broadsided. Unfortunately, I was not wearing my seat belt and was ejected from my car.

I landed in a ditch. My injuries were critical: a severed trachea, two collapsed lungs, a fractured left shoulder blade, five broken ribs, a small fracture in my back, a torn anterior cruciate ligament in my right knee, a fractured right fibula, and a sprained wrist.

Immediately after the accident, I knew I was starting at ground zero. I was busy trying to overcome the physical limitations caused by the accident when the emotional pain suddenly began. For one, the psychological damage I suffered from made it difficult for me to get back into a car. Suffice it to say, the damages I suffered both mentally and physically would take a lot of time and effort to heal from. I wanted to recover as quickly as possible, but eventually I had to accept that the healing process would not be completed overnight. My future in the NBA was at risk during my rehabilitation. Once I did come back, I felt like I did as much as I could to close the gap between my abilities before the accident and after.

While rehabilitating from my injury, I felt overwhelmed by my demons. In hindsight, I should have sought out psychological assistance for my emotional scars.

I felt lost trying to get back to the NBA. Returning to the game was such a humbling experience that I was almost in tears because of my poor playing. I considered hanging up my professional career, but my athletic drive would not let me. I fixed my game through intense workouts with my father. I realized I would not be the same player as I had been prior to the accident, but it did not mean I should give up. I knew when I went to play that I needed to be happy with my progress because I was playing to the best of my ability. Unfortunately, it was not enough to get back to the player I used to be. So, I retired in 2000 and attempted different ventures. Nonetheless, I was haunted for a long time by the traumatic accident and the loss of my NBA career. Like any athlete, I became lost. Over time, I found a new calling in the sports field, eventually becoming a highly successful coach at Arizona State University.

If I could give advice to other injured athletes, I would say: "There is no playbook." Athletes should try to be as well-rounded as they can because the reality is that there will be an end to their sports careers. Develop other interests and passions so that if your biggest passion falls apart, you can shift gears and find something else that fulfills you. Despite finding new interests in my life outside of playing, I still wish that I had been able to stop playing on my own terms.

I have accepted that playing basketball just was not my journey. Coaching has become my passion now, and I wish I had gotten into it earlier because it has helped me heal many of my wounds. Once I was motivated to get back into the game, I realized that motivation was inherent within me, and it would help me transition into coaching. I got entrenched in developing players. I studied game films over and over and knew that this would be my next calling.

The impact of sports psychology and using as many resources as possible benefits the athlete. During my rehabilitation, I did not share a lot of my emotional grief because I thought I could handle it. In hindsight, I should have invested some time in speaking to someone. In my mind, I had to be tough, so that's what stopped me from saying much about my injuries. As I see it now, the use of sports psychology techniques is a valuable tool for athletes.

This is not uncommon. All athletes deal with the loss of sport in different ways, and many fall into self-destructive behaviors. Some succumb to them while others, like the athletes in this book, have been able to find a better path. How they came to lead a better life is what I ultimately wanted to share in this book.

Not surprisingly, intercollegiate, amateur, and professional athletes whose sport careers were ended prematurely by injury or for other reasons have experienced less life fulfillment than those whose careers were not terminated prematurely. This can be dependent on many factors. In my own experience, at the time of my injury and for about fifteen years after, there was nobody who could make the pain go away and no one who could understand what I was experiencing unless they had walked through the fire with me.

One time, I remember being in the athletic training room at Arizona State University going through physical therapy when my buddy Tarence Wheeler looked at me and said, "Nobody knows what we are going through." That was not a "woe is me" cry; it was the true internal pain of an athlete. This was an athlete with a promising basketball career. The physical therapist and trainers could see what we were going through, but could they feel it with their hearts? Could they really understand it if they had never gone through it? They could not possibly relate to the darkness that fills the injured athlete's mind unless they too had gone through a similar experience.

CHAPTER FOUR

THE INJURY

"Without sports to help define or evaluate themselves, many athletes are left confused as to their identities, low in self-esteem and confidence."[8]

There is no easy way to tell an athlete that their injury is career ending; this is our greatest fear. Although it will not change the outcome, the way the message is conveyed can greatly affect the mental state of the athlete. Although this was more common years ago, sports medicine doctors will still tell injured athletes without a blink of an eye, "Your career is over," or "You will never be the same." Often, doctors do not realize that those words can last as a traumatic memory for these athletes. It is imperative that doctors show empathy in their doctor- patient dialogue and the delivery of such devastating news.

There is an approach to telling someone that what they love the most has been compromised. The residual effect of hearing such devastating news is usually psychological because, to be a great athlete, you have to be strong-willed and strong-minded. This is something that is demonstrated in the story of Vinny Paz in the movie *In the Bleed.* Vinny was a world champion boxer who was in a horrific car accident that left him with a broken neck. When he was in the hospital, the doctor emotionally and reluctantly had to tell him that his fighting career was over and that he may never walk again. This particular doctor displayed empathy when telling Paz that he would never box again. Paz was devastated and thought, "What else could I do if I am not boxing? He was a fighter, that was all he had known. He refused to believe that he could not fight again, so he persisted through his

---

8.   Crook and Robertson, "Transitions Out of Elite Sport."

injury and boxed for twelve more years after he had been told his career was over. Although the odds were against him, Paz found the physical and mental fortitude to push on. He fought two years later, not only making it through the match but recapturing the title too. It takes tremendous determination to push through that pain. Mentally, he was ready, but everyone around him was worried about what it would be like if he was injured for good. Paz just thought about how his life would play out if he didn't get back in the ring, and how he used to be world champ. For some athletes like Paz, this is what a "fighter" is; this was his instinct. He told the doctor that he would box again, and he did.

Doctors, of course, have to err on the side of caution. They are taught to diagnose, treat, and rehabilitate, but often are not taught how to approach someone with news of their serious injury. They don't understand that telling an athlete that their career is over is essentially a death sentence.

When I lived in Connecticut and was the manager for the Sports Injury Prevention Program for the Connecticut Children's Medical Center, I would go out and give talks to sports medicine and orthopedic doctors about how to break the news to athletes when they are injured. A sprained ankle that can sideline a young athlete for six weeks during a ten-week season can be devastating. How the news is broken is something that needs to be reviewed, and the presentation should be reconsidered. Of course, this does not apply to all. However, it should be known that athletes hone in on every word said to them, and those words can be carried with them for a lifetime. It can be devastating if doctors do not carefully consider how the message is conferred. I once witnessed a doctor tell a young, promising baseball pitcher, "Sorry your season is over; at least you have next year." That news is devastating, especially to an athlete who would be heavily recruited during their junior year. Many doctors have not been athletes, so they do not understand how that kind of news can crush an athlete's psyche. When I interviewed John Mishock, he talked about how doctors place a label on these athletes in regard to their injury. The label is the specific injury that these athletes have, and once these athletes hear that label, they feel defeated.

When interviewing Dr. John Mishock, I was elated when he told me that he does not label an athlete's injury, as he feels it can stifle their mental and physical recovery.

JOHN MISHOCK, PT, DPT, DC:

I am a former baseball player who played as an outfielder in college. I had a dream of playing in the pros, but my career was inundated with elbow and shoulder injuries. While injured, I became quite frustrated because baseball was my life. After I could no longer play, I became depressed over the injury and struggled with overcoming my identity as a baseball player. After a long battle to find a new path in life, I decided to pursue a career in physical therapy and chiropractic medicine.

Working in physical therapy and chiropractic medicine is what I was meant to do. I became empowered by my career and sought to help other athletes. The suffering I endured from the loss of being a player set the ground-work for what I am meant to be doing now. I allowed my mental toughness that was inspired by my love of the game to translate into my new career. I now work with young athletes, where I assist them in handling their rehabilitation and letting them know that their injuries do not define them.

From my experiences working in physical therapy, I have noticed that athletes who have come into my office are clearly bothered by how doctors "labeled" their injuries. My job is to make the young athletes realize that they should not label themselves by their injuries because they can overcome their physical effects. I do not want other athletes to suffer the same identity crisis that I did as a young, injured athlete, and so I show athletes today that their "you can't stop me" mentality can be used for more than just athletics. The pain of losing your career never goes away, but there are other passions outside the world of sports that can be just as fulfilling.

My buddy Tarence Wheeler was the Pac-10 Player of the Year as a freshman, but the following year he suffered an almost career-ending PCL (Posterior Cruciate Ligament) injury. After the injury, he fought to come back to preserve his promising college and possible professional career He lost his opportunity to go pro in the States, but he was later able to play in Europe. That injury, however, took away that once fast first step (his quickness) and confidence that had left players looking back for their shorts.

TARENCE WHEELER

I was a Division I basketball player at ASU. At the time, I was a leader of the team and the best in scoring and assists up to my junior year. During the opening game at the Pac-10, I took one step and was injured. The trainer, Sarge, took me to the training room, felt my left leg, and told me that I would be out for a year with an injured PCL. I broke down in tears when the news broke. I was not prepared for such a loss. To make matters worse, I would sit in my apartment depressed with no one to check on me. I was on an island by myself, slipping more into depression and losing contact with my teammates.

If it had not been for this trainer from ASU, I would not have been able to return to play at the level I did. Sarge had developed a program outside of the physical therapist. At six o'clock every morning, we would train in the water for thirty minutes. Sarge was a guardian angel to allow me to play again. Back then, there was no support for mental performance, making me feel like I was being treated like "shit." My coaches wanted me to come back to play six months later, but I knew I was not ready. I told the coach that my life was not centered around basketball and I wanted a future where I could walk and run at the age of fifty. I lost trust in my coaches after that point, realizing that they cared more for my talent than my well-being.

I came back next year and led my team to the NCAA tournament where we won a game in March Madness. After that, I tried out for the Suns and Pacers. Eventually, I played in Brazil, Argentina, and Venezuela for ten years in international ball.

During my second year in Venezuela, I accepted that this would be my future, but it hurt me not to know what would have happened had I not been injured. Believing that there was nothing else for me to do, I felt socially dead when I stopped playing ball.

By now, you may be asking yourself: How was my transition into nonathletic life after playing ball for ten years? While searching for what to do next, I was always told to "Use basketball and don't let basketball use you."

I was now able to help younger players. My mission now is to keep them in school and out of trouble. Basketball prepared me for tough times and how to reinvent myself—how to get confidence back with the ebb and flow of life. Basketball assisted me in handling tough times. I was prepared to get along with most people due to playing ball and handling others personally.

Today, I work as a community activist that places young people in positions to be successful. I am a very proactive worker in my community in Detroit. Kids need a chance to love themselves beyond their mistakes and be given opportunities for internships and job training. Don't fall into the trap of how you were raised. It is easy to be conditioned if you come from a lower socioeconomic status. However, I learned how to persevere and overcome the traps by finding an outlet through a sport like basketball that helped me become successful.

Another friend of mine, a college quarterback, was sidelined by a mental injury of frustration and sadness after he stopped playing. For him, the transition of no longer being a competitive athlete was traumatic. He never spoke of it, but I could see and feel his pain; I felt it too as an athlete. This person could have made it to the pros, but he got lost in the shuffle. Watching his old college films made him break down and sob. The dream haunted him then and probably will continue to do so for the rest of his life. However, he never would admit the pain, it just laid within him. For a while, he tried to hide by using drinking and gambling to deal with the depression that had set in.

Even though he kept playing to keep the dream alive, he never ended up where he always wanted and deserved to be. He also never dealt with the pain, and it hurt him. I do not know where he is now, but for the time I knew him, he worked hard and never wanted to find normalcy in the real world because he was an athlete at heart. He needed the feeling of competition. He had been extremely unsuccessful outside of the sports environment. He loved to play football and that was all that mattered to him. It is a tough realization for athletes to admit that when their career is over, they are not certain how they will move on. My friend's path of avoiding responsibility, indulging in various destructive activities to ease the pain, and hating himself is, unfortunately, not unusual for athletes like him.

Anyone whose career has ended still has that inner drive. We all have different mental capabilities to overcome certain events. When there is a life-changing event, it takes time to process emotions, determine what the next step is, and take that step to figure out what will assist us over the hurdle.

Historically, the premise behind athletes being paid well was that if they did become injured or debilitated, they could have the money to survive into their future and take care of their families. However, salaries have gotten out of control over the past few decades; it has changed the game. For someone who has a pure love for sports and has lost everything they worked for, it is tough to stomach.

Not all athletes who end their career or are injured become devastated. There are a small few who are happy to end their careers and take on different ventures, but this is not the case for those who feel that failure is not an option. Unfortunately, that is often how athletes view the end of their career when it has been cut short.

When the passion for a sport runs so deep it just becomes a piece of who you are, that is the psyche of an athlete. Samantha McKay is a perfect example of a player who plays for the love of the game.

SAMANTHA MCKAY

I was a basketball player for the University of Dayton. When I was twenty-two years old, I signed to play Euro league in Hungary in 2013. A month into my first season overseas, I was on a bus headed to a game when the bus got hit and rolled off the highway. Most of the team landed outside the bus, while some were stuck inside. My general manager lay lifeless next to me, and the head coach was also dead. I had three fractures in my neck, a broken foot, fractured ribs, and road burn that covered a good portion of my back. The accident left me in shock and in great pain, but I had to help other players who were seriously wounded. In order to assist them, I attempted to crawl toward them until an innocent civilian stopped me and laid me back against the ditch.

Right after the accident, I felt more messed up mentally than physically. The accident was completely surreal, and I had many psychological obstacles to overcome afterword. After seven months of being in a neck brace, I went back to Hungary in order to start my journey back to the court. However, very quickly I learned that this was going to be a very vigorous rehabilitation. Mentally, I was worried about how I would perform after rehab. I went to California to work with a former trainer to help me rehabilitate. She was my lifeline; without her I would not be the player or person I am today. I went back to play again the next year in Hungary, then France, and then Estonia.

In 2016, I got injured after getting T-boned in a car accident in Philadelphia. Physically, the injuries were not as severe as the first accident. Mentally, the injuries were drastic. But again, I found my way back to the court. Another year in Estonia, before moving to Greece. I finally felt that I was back to the player I wanted to be until I suffered another injury, this time on the court. I broke my ankle, but stubbornly endured the pain and continued to play. It was not until after this injury that I began to see how much my psyche had changed. The emotional side effects of my injuries never really came into play until I chose to deal with them. These side effects included bouts of undiagnosed depression. At the time, I thought that I was tired, but I could not figure out why. I believe that when someone no longer has a specific goal to aim for, they become fatigued by the subconscious emotional turbulence. We can easily get fatigued by the mental strain of an injury. In my opinion, the Injured Athletic Questionnaire should be a validated tool because of how long it took me to realize how profoundly affected I was by the mental fatigue of my injuries without this support.

A lot of athletes, whether they know it or not, struggle with anxiety from the stress that is placed on them. My anxiety was caused by the multitude of traumatic events that have occurred in my life. In the first accident, I did not feel that I had choice but to come back because many of my teammates were not able to play again. Despite some trepidations, I convinced myself that I had to play for the teammates who no longer could. It took me a while to find a balance between my personal and athletic lives, but I did eventually find that balance thanks to the psychological tools from a sports psychologist at the University of Dayton sports program.

Survivor's guilt haunted me after the accident. I was fortunate because I quickly identified with this condition and found support from a cultivated community at Dayton. They sent me letters and t-shirts to show their support. That support unquestionably helped me get through my injury and find my desire to play again. The fans meant so much to me and reached out to assist me with whatever I needed.

I believe that athletes know who will help them get through their injuries. For me, my strong connection with my fans fuels my passion for playing. Without this connection and support, I may not have recovered as well as I did. This support has been a pillar of my strength.

There is not enough that can be said for social support. It empowers athletes and helps them feel that someone has their back when they are going through tough times.

> I no longer feel like I have to play for anyone else. I used to carry my supporters and the weight of my injured teammates with me no matter what, but this burden was both beneficial and detrimental.
>
> I will be playing this upcoming year, 2020-2021 in Greece for my fourth consecutive season. The outside pressures will no longer affect me because my desire to play comes purely from my love of the game.

Samantha is still playing and plans to compete in Greece next year. The outside pressures will no longer affect her because her desire to play comes purely from her love of basketball. The participation in highly organized, competitive athletics demands time, energy, and commitments that constitute a major focus in the lives of many adolescents and adults. Considering the years of commitment that are reflected in the sports careers of many athletes, playing up to one's potential and realizing the best results of one's investment may have psychological effects extending beyond an athlete's playing days. "Some athletes who have sustained a career-ending injury before completing eligibility showed significantly lower life satisfaction than those who had not."[9] This goes back to the discussion of the loss of identity and confidence that sports had brought to these athletes. Moreover,

---

9.   Douglas Kleiber et al., "Quality of Exit from University Sports and Life Satisfaction in Early Adulthood," *Sociology of Sport Journal* 4, no. 1 (1987): 28–36.

self-perceived success as well as recognition and visibility, particularly during the final phases of one's career, may affect how an athlete reacts to the transition out of sport.

DEALING WITH INJURY

Why is loss of identity so painful? When athletes are mentally or physically injured, they feel stressed, confused, and fearful of a complete loss of the season and possibly their career.

When something so personal, something you have dedicated such hard work and sacrificed so much for, is taken away, it is a loss like no other; a loss of one's self. More often than not, in order for something to be fixed physically, it first needs to be fixed mentally and emotionally. This will promote the healing of one's psyche and ultimately the body.

There are a wide variety of emotions that come after a loss. It is imperative that athletes come to terms with their losses and learn to accept that their careers are over. For an athlete whose entire life has revolved around sports, it is extremely difficult to emotionally readjust. Thoughts must be restructured in order to adapt and move forward. Some athletes can do it themselves in their own time, while others are so grief-stricken that they need to seek assistance. There is nothing wrong with seeking help. In fact, it is the person who realizes they cannot do it alone who is strong and, on their way, to healing their psyche.

Suicide is a reality among athletes who lose their careers suddenly due to an injury or retirement. It is important for an athlete to know that the anger they feel can be misdirected inward and sometimes cannot be identified as depression. Sometimes a person can hurt so much and feel so much pain that it comes out through anger that manifests itself as destructive behaviors and, ultimately, suicidal thoughts.

One of the main challenges incurred by athletes is the lack of emotional evaluation before the physical assessment. In order to heal, both the body and mind must be worked on from the start. Athletes tend to fall into such a situational depression that they often do not realize it is happening. Looking back to when I was first injured, the devastating sadness caused me to pull away from my teammates and coach. When the doctor told me that I could never play basketball again, I felt alone and like no one could understand what had just happened to me. With a cold and emotionless response, one doctor had just changed the course of my entire life. He also told me that my injury could affect my ability to have children. I was young and naïve, so I believed him.

In one doctor's appointment, the thing I loved to do was taken away from me. I did not want to believe it and went to six other doctors hoping it was not true. Back then, a back injury, especially for a young lady, was a big deal because most women were expected to have children and would need a strong back for childbearing. At least, that is the way it was put to me. It scared me because I wanted to be a mom one day. Coach McHugh struggled with the news and was angry at the doctors, but they had spoken to my parents by then and that was that. So, I listened to the doctor as he would not clear me to play at ASU, and by the middle of my sophomore year, my college basketball career was over. In my mind, so was my life. It's amazing how a doctor would never say that today, and I'm happy to see that women's athletics have come so far.

Depression can occur when there is a disruption to a lifestyle that helps define a person's worth. An athletic injury may prevent sports participation without noticeably affecting other areas of an individual's life. It is hypothesized that individuals who derive their self-worth solely from their identity as an athlete are at an increased risk for depression after experiencing an athletic injury.[10]

Then, grief sets in. An athlete who no longer competes begins to feel as if there is nothing left to do, thus reducing self-esteem as if they were not good enough and will not find success in the real world. Many athletes are just not taught the tools to deal with the world outside sports. They do not realize that the valuable mental tools they inherited from athletic participation can be applied to help ease the transition to a life without sport.

The experience of loss is painful and generates feelings of grief. To athletes, grieving is a private matter. Grief is not a single emotion, but a series of phases through which a mourner passes. It is the response of the body, mind, and soul to intolerable pain and despair. "Grief involves a deep sense of loss and helplessness."[11] We would be fooling ourselves to think that anyone who works for something and then loses it will not take time to experience the process of grieving. Sometimes, athletes cannot get out of the dark hole

---

10. B. Brewer, "Self-Identity and Specific Vulnerability to Depressed Mood," *Journal of Personality* 3, no. 61 (1993): 344–54.

11. David B. Cohen, *Out of the Blue: Depression and Human Nature* (New York: Norton and Company, 1994): 65.

they find themselves in after their sport is over. A perfect example would be former Phoenix Cardinals player Louis Sharp. Once Sharp retired, he ended up in and out of jail due to drug problems. It is sad that after his sport ended, Sharp was not provided with the tools to acclimate back into the real world. The life of a professional athlete is not the same as that of some person who is working a nine-to-five job. Most of these athletes lose their friends, their lifestyles, and, with that, their self-worth.

KNOW YOUR WORTH

Some people only identify as being an athlete. Sometimes, as athletes, we can be so confident on the field or court that when we are off it, we do not quite know how to navigate our lives. When I was playing, I was so confident. When I was injured, I lost who I was and all my confidence with it. It took me almost dying in a hospital from a surgery in 2017 (at almost forty-six years old) to realize what I am, who I am, and what I want to be. I have worked with athletes for over twenty years. I have taught, coached, and counseled them. My mission is to empower them and provide them with the tools they need to realize who they are now and what their worth is.

I was always too worried about the next ten years. My mother would tell me that if it were up to me, I would have the next ten years planned out on my calendar. Well, there is an old saying, "Man plans, God laughs." I, like many others, learned that the hard way.

Through my experiences, I learned to control what I can, and now I pass that same lesson on to my athletes. I teach them to discover what makes them tick and have it transcend their sport to apply to so many other aspects of their lives. It is important to give 150 percent to everything you do to help you transition into a life away from sports.

As people, we are always evolving. Personally, I am still a work in progress due to the loss of basketball so many years ago. I would be lying if I said that the loss of my basketball career did not still hurt, but we all have a cross to bear. This loss has changed me in so many ways, but I've become stronger because of it. I have never and will never give up. My mantra is: "I will not be broken!"—not physically, mentally, or emotionally. Life has tried to break me, but I have overcome, and if I can pass along even some of this knowledge and experience to my athletes, I will.

Knowing your worth includes so much more than confidence. It means empowering yourself and believing that you can achieve anything, even after loss. There is always something else to conquer and to achieve. People will attempt to break you, but you must step right past them. Life was meant to be lived. It was meant to be felt, and we were meant to thrive. We all have an inner strength; we just tap into it at different junctures in our lives. Nonetheless, the goal is to always find our way. It does not matter how old you are when you do; the point is that we live before we die.

CHAPTER FIVE

ATHLETIC IDENTITY

"Athletic identity is described as the degree to which an individual identifies with the athlete role and looks to others for acknowledgement of that role."[12]

Athletes tie who they are to their sport and it becomes an identifying factor on the evolution of their self-concept. Athletes are a different breed, and they know it. This is not to say that they are better than nonathletes, just that their minds work differently. They are pressure cookers, but it is not the same pressure as on Wall Street. The difference is that on Wall Street, you know there is pressure, and when practicing as an athlete, the pressure comes and goes. The expectations are higher, and the potential is limitless. There really is no mountain high enough for a true competitive athlete.

The physical pain athletes endure along with the mental and emotional strain is tremendous, and if they are told that their career is over, it can be a ridiculously hard pill to swallow.

"Sometimes an athlete can fall prey not just to the injury itself, but to the emotional trauma that surrounds it."[13]

This quote is so powerful to me because I have experienced it firsthand. I would be screaming and crying inside, but no one would know. I had lost my family—my teammates—and consequently, myself. It is a very intimate loss, and it can take years to find oneself again. It took me at least fifteen years, but the pain has truly never gone away. I do not know why,

---

12.   B. Brewer, J. Van Raalte, and D. Linder, "Athletic Identity: Hercules' Muscles or Achilles Heel?," *International Journal of Sport Psychology* 24 (1993); 237–54.

13.   John Heil, *Psychology of Sport Injury* (Human Kinetics: 1993).

but I do know that I still have that inner fire burning inside me to be the best at whatever I take on. An identity crisis does not discriminate; it is at its peak when an athlete's career is over or ends abruptly. Why is it that some athletes become so lost? The problem lies within the psyche, subconscious, and soul, because some of these issues run so deep it can take time for sports psychologists find answers and solutions. It all depends on the athlete and their personality characteristics. After a career-ending injury, an athlete feels that they are no longer recognized as the athlete they once were and that they are no longer accepted by anyone or anything. They need to figure out who they are and how to fit into society as someone other than themselves, the athlete. The question becomes: if I am not playing my sport, then who am I now? Jackie Ryan, Allen Watson, and I, to name a few, have all felt this way. Most of the athletes that I have spoken to have discussed how they continued on by either coaching or helping others. They found the social aspect of being an athlete created a skill set and the mental fortitude to find something that would bring both fulfillment and success. So, that constant question of "Who am I?" can become the statement, "Look at me now!"

STAKING CLAIM IN YOUR IDENTITY

Self-concepts develop over time and can be increased with success in the athletic domain, thus influencing self-esteem and motivation. Participating in sport can assist athletes to gain necessary confidence as their athletic abilities increase. Once athletes have a taste of success, they are driven to work harder over time. Then when they see the benefits of their hard work, it is easy for them to identify themselves with their sport and as an athlete.

It seems that a career-ending injury will complicate the self-identity of the athlete. The bottom line is that an athlete who holds all the eggs of their identity in the athlete basket may in fact be in for an emotional disturbance at the time of a serious injury. Most athletes feel that they were involved in sports because they enjoyed them, they were good at them, and they mitigated the realities of life, making everything better to deal with. For the most part, the pressures athletes know best are competitive pressures. Reality is another story.

Some athletes have no choice; they feel their sport is a way to a better life, the frog that must be kissed to receive a prize. It becomes the sole dream for some kind of achievement. To put it simply, athletes believe success will lead to glory.

Most athletes do not prepare themselves for career alternatives. There is a large percentage of athletes who are attending college just so they can be playing. While to some a degree is equally as important, it is still not as important as what happens after college. This lack of preparation can have a traumatic effect on an athlete who loses their career early. This is why the mind and body psychological perspectives are so important when training athletes. Providing mental preparedness assists athletes with life's obstacles once the competition stops.

The main point here is that unless you dig really deep within yourself, do you truly know what you are made of? Maybe that loss happened for a reason—to help you find yourself and not stake claim in the identity of whatever it is you are doing. Find worth and self-confidence within yourself to succeed in your next journey.

ATHLETIC ADVANTAGE

As previously mentioned, some athletes tend to lack foresight into the mental preparation that is necessary to prevail in their post-athletic careers due to the athletic advantage. The athletic advantage occurs when people "help" athletes by giving them special privileges. It starts at school, where teachers and instructors sometimes choose to make exceptions for athletes to assist them in passing their classes more easily because their workout regimens are usually a full load.

Athletes are the center of attention once they receive a scholarship and participate at an institution. Their class schedule is made for them, and most of their daily decisions along with that. They do not develop the coping skills necessary to deal with other life stressors when a traumatic event such as an injury takes place within their athletic career. They have received so much that it has been to their detriment as they have been deprived of specific learning skills other "normal" students have; this also carries into athletes' professional careers. This is the privilege of the sports world.

Most collegiate athletes go to class in the morning, then to the training room to get taped or receive any kind of physical therapy they might need, and finally they are off to practice. After practice, they eat and go to study hall. By the time they make it to the study hall, it is usually ten at night. Quite often, athletes' lives are pampered because their school schedules are designed for them to meet the needs of their sports. Since athletes do not have to do too much on their own, a silent codependence is formed. Unfortunately, for most athletes whose careers end early, they find out how dependent they really are when trying to find a job or deal with other life intricacies.

Athletes are often allowed and even encouraged to remain dependent on sport administrators and coaches for decision-making. As a result, this may leave them weak in the self-management skills that are important in alternate and future career decisions.

The socialization required to transition from being an athlete to a "normal" person is difficult. A new social role has to be established, and along with that comes a new identity. Different jobs and different educational endeavors can hopefully put the puzzle back together. Athletes have the mentality of always trying to succeed, so they struggle later with the realization that they have to wait their turn no matter how hard they work. As an athlete, you do not have to wait your turn if you can get the job done better than anyone else—you go straight to the top. In the real world, hard work does not always pay off. There is sometimes a ladder to climb.

In my experience, athletes who reach the peak of their personal achievements early in life might have a painful or traumatic retirement experience because no other activity would ensure the same social and personal reverence that sports does. As a consequence, it is possible that these athletes will never find an undertaking to replace the feelings created by their sport, and the loss of praise and acknowledgment will contribute to difficulty adjusting out of sport.

THE DISPLACED ATHLETE

Maybe it was not about basketball after all. Perhaps, I should put more value in the lessons I was able to take from the game and translate them into real life. Being an athlete taught me how to persevere under stressful situations, it taught me how to be a team player and taught me to work hard and be disciplined.

When you leave the world of an athlete and have to get out into the workplace, the social life is completely different; it is altogether a whole new kind of competition. You will no longer have the type of family you have worked hard with, practiced with, and sacrificed with. Personally, I never felt like I belonged. It then becomes an inner struggle just to re-light the fire that once burned inside. It is like a severed relationship, meaning that the transition is not easy. Going from the world of a competitive athlete into the "normal" world can be tough. However, moving forward and finding success can be fulfilling also. It does take time, but it is possible. For an injured athlete, the grieving process results from a loss of one's self. This grief can potentially stifle success when mainstreaming into the unathletic world. But there is always light at the end of the tunnel.

Because of all of the sacrifice, respect, hard work, and confidence, the athlete who has to move into their new life will often feel displaced. They are only familiar with the family of athletes they have competed with.

Sometimes, after the transition out of sports, athletes feel like they are socially dead. They may feel displaced when they enter life among nonathletic people. It becomes emotionally troublesome for some athletes to overcome their identity as an athlete. This goes back to the question: "If I am not a player, then who am I?" More often than not, athletes will struggle with this reality and succumb to trouble pursuing other career venues.

Bobby Hurley Jr. is a perfect example of this. When I interviewed him, he had discussed trying different things. He was not certain what he wanted to do. It is not uncommon for an athlete to feel displaced while trying to find their new situation in life.

CHAPTER SIX

HOW CAN SPORTS MEDICINE EXPEDITE THE HEALING PROCESS?

"In order to heal the body, the mind must be calmed."[14] The rehabilitation process for athletes who are injured is complicated. Just because an athlete's sports career has ended does not mean that the rehabilitation process should not be handled in a manner that assists them. The first step is to be able to help the athlete find peace within their mind by properly informing and educating the athlete of their injury and what the rehabilitation will entail. The athlete must believe that they will be better and will heal. This gives the athlete back the sense of control they felt they lost due to injury.

Typically, at the initial stage of injury, the body and mind are at a complete disconnect. The athlete first does not want to believe that this has happened to them, and the afterthoughts can create doubt in their mind. At this juncture, it is imperative that someone assist the athlete with mental recovery. Building the body to become stronger physically is not enough if the mind does not become stronger too. The strength to endure rehabilitation comes from one's inner self. It is the process of building fortitude within the heart, soul, and mind.

For example, Patricia Boyd, a childhood friend, is an Ironman. The night before the Lake Placid Ironman in 2017, she broke her toe. Now, anyone who has broken a toe and walked on it knows that the pain can be excruciating. The pain from a broken toe can also mess with one's mind. Yes, it was just a toe, but when you are running and biking for a series of sixty-plus miles, it can become a mental impediment. Patricia, a true champion, completed the competition while

---

14. Miele, *L.(2020)*

just pushing the pain aside as well as experiencing two flats tires on her ride. The mind-body component cannot be underestimated. Harnessing the strength of the mind and the proper use of the mental tools it takes to push the physical and psychological pain aside is a great feat.

Sports medicine has made great advances in the physical rehabilitation of injured athletes, but little attention has been given to the mental side of this recovery process. Rehabilitation is a process, both psychologically and physically. Mental preparations in recovery are generally underused because many athletes and rehabilitation professionals lack training, and common usage of psychological interventions are sporadic. Sports medicine specialists, trainers, and coaches would do well to identify certain behaviors indicative of possible psychological distress, especially when dealing with an injury. Once injured, athletes must be aware of the severity of the injury, the length of time to expect to be out of play, and what it will take for them to return both physically and mentally to their prior competition level.

For decades, interventions have been used to help injured athletes who require surgery. At times, sports psychologists have employed interventions involving sport injuries. These specific interventions are sometimes deemed necessary to accelerate the overall healing and rehabilitation process. Injuries in sports appear to be increasing in frequency, and research into the psychological aspects of athletic injuries continues to gain popularity within the sports psychology and training literature. A serious injury can be both physically and psychologically debilitating for the sports participant, especially when the athlete begins to question their return to athletic activities.

Many of these athletes have said that the period following surgery was like being in their own personal hell—a place where no one could possibly understand the physical and emotional work they have ahead of them to return to play. Athletes who are injured often feel tremendous loss, and the uncertainty of recovery can weigh heavily in their minds. To be injured is a great setback for that individual's hopes, plans, lifestyle, physical environment, and social contacts. These feelings are also experienced by former athletes who have maintained their athleticism if they become injured in their late thirties or forties. It seems that with any injury comes pain, and with pain comes fluctuating emotions.

One consistent emotion that factors into the athlete's recovery is anxiety. Anxiety and depression can be conceptualized in a number of ways, and outcome variables typically include the psychological, behavioral, and physiological. For example, stress may lead to an increase in muscle tension that can change flexibility, poor oxygen flow, and poor circulation, making it more difficult for the athlete to recuperate quickly.

Injury triggers a wide range of emotions that progress through various stages similar to Elizabeth Kubler-Ross's five stages of grief.[15]

-Denial
-Anger
-Bargaining
-Depression
-Acceptance

---

15.   Elizabeth Kubler-Ross, *On Death and Dying* (New York: McMillan, 1969).

ACCEPTANCE AND REORGANIZATION

When an athlete has a strong identity, they sometimes become disoriented; they mentally evaluate why this may have happened to them. It is in this state that they will experience some or all of the five stages of grief. When, at their own pace, athletes finally accept that their future has taken a different turn, they learn to accept it and move on to reorganizing their life plan.

PROPER SCREENING QUESTIONS FOR PTS & ATCS

When an athlete comes into a clinic and seems down or sad about an injury, the Physical Therapists (PTs) and Certified Athletic Trainers (ATCs) who are assisting them should take note. The first question that should come to mind is: Will this athlete be hindered psychologically by this injury? I have seen firsthand how psychological well-being can play a large factor in adherence to the rehabilitation program.[16] Even if the athlete is no longer able to compete, they still need to be physically functional for their daily life. They will still need to become strong enough to overcome the physical pain by using mental skill sets to assist them.

The next question for PTs and ATCs is how to get these inured athletes in touch with a sports psychology consultant. Many athletes feel that if they seek help, they are being weak,

---

16. Laura Miele, "Vancouver Olympics 2010: How Can We Give Athletes an Edge on Injury Rehabilitation?" *Podium Sports Journal* (2010), accessed Dec 22, 2020, https://www.podiumsportsjournal.com/2010/02/17/vancouver-olympics-2010-how-can-we-give-athletes-an-edge-on-injury-rehabilitation/.

which serves as another indication they will be viewed as vulnerable and not likely to "bounce back." Some may feel that there is really nothing mentally wrong with them and the only problem is the physical injury itself.

Athletes are quite often nervous about their injuries, surgery, and what rehabilitation may entail. Another reaction to anxiety can cause the athlete to retreat emotionally and become depressed. There are important warning signs to notice if you think an athlete you are working with is going through a depressive state:

1) Loss of appetite
2) Emotional withdrawal
3) Social withdrawal
4) Indifference to their rehabilitation
5) Spending extra time in the training room after each session.

Anxiety and depression can cause distortions in the athletes' thinking processes. At times, these cognitive distortions can seriously impair the recovery process. Some athletes may feel like they cannot go on. They want to give up because they see no light at the end of the tunnel. They may feel as if they will never be physically healthy again. Cognitive distortions like these have been known to lead to substance abuse. If pronounced enough, these distortions can become delusional and contribute to possible suicide. Every PT and ATC should have a certified sport psychologist at the ready for referral in these situations. Consultants are sometimes trained in sports sciences, while others come from clinical backgrounds and are licensed therapists.

Often, friends and family surrounding the athlete notice the emotional change before the athlete realizes it. This is the time when someone needs to step in and bring it to the athlete's attention, which can be difficult and is sometimes not welcomed. The bottom line is this: athletes need to focus on healing their minds first, emotionally prepare themselves for the trials ahead, and accept the rehabilitation process. Once they can get past that hurdle, the physical healing can begin. Too often, athletes are far into the rehabilitation process before they realize how much anxiety, depression, and frustration have sidetracked their focus. They may isolate themselves from friends and family and believe their rehabilitation is not progressing as well as they initially hoped.

QUESTIONS ATHLETES SHOULD BE ASKING

Dealing and coping with an injury can be problematic for an athlete. Sometimes athletes do not ask enough questions because they do not want to know the answers. Sometimes they are placed into a surgical situation so quickly that they do not have the time to process what just happened, much less what lies ahead with regard to pain, rehabilitation, and return to play. The main concerns on most athletes' minds are "When can I play again?" and "Will I ever be the same as I was?"

In the *Journal of Athletic Training*, there was a statement suggesting that PTs and ATCs were in the "best position to educate athletes on the use of psychological interventions to enhance the recovery process"[17] It is true that PTs and ATCs have the most exposure to the emotional side of the athlete. However, unless they have been properly trained to address the emotional aspects of recovery, they should seek out a sports psychology consultant for this type of assistance. PTs and ATCs are clearly the best suited to educate and treat the athlete for an injury, yet it also makes sense for them to consult collaboratively with both the athlete's coach and the sports psychologist so they can set goals and employ longer-term strategies consistent with the athlete's background. This can provide a structure and format familiar to the athlete, so they have goals, learning objectives, training targets, and more to look forward to each week.

CALLING FOR AN ASSESSMENT TOOL

The most important moment in time for an injured athlete is when they first enter rehabilitation. At this juncture, it is difficult to determine how emotionally and psychologically affected by the injury that athlete may be. Although assessment tools are used for many different situations, targeted assessments can greatly facilitate the rehabilitation process.

An assessment tool that properly identifies athletes who may struggle emotionally and psychologically with their injuries would likely prove quite helpful to many PTs and

---

17. J. Jordan Hamson-Utley, Scott Martin, and Jason Walters, "Athletic Trainers' and Physical Therapists' Perceptions of the Effectiveness of Psychological Skills Within Sport Injury Rehabilitation Programs," *Journal of Athletic Training* 43, no. 3 (2008):258–64.

ATCs. This assessment would be used as a screening tool in orthopedic sports medicine rehabilitation clinics to identify factors that might help or hinder the recovery process of an athlete. Given the various stages in recovery and the various benchmarks, both physical and mental, that must be met, a strong understanding of each athlete's rehabilitative mindset can be pivotal in managing rehabilitation.

For example, if athletes suffer from depression, not only does this cause a possible setback in adherence to rehabilitation, but it can negatively and substantially impact the emotional and psychological state of an athlete.

I have created the Injured Athlete Questionnaire (IAQ) to be a tool to assist in the discovery of situational depression. It is imperative that someone dealing with an injury heal their mind, because it will allow for a faster rehabilitation process. I was able to identify this in the athletes I have worked with in the Elite Sports Medicine physical therapy room at the Connecticut Children's Medical Center. After creating this assessment tool (see Appendix), I began to use it for pilot research until the program was dropped due to budget cuts and I could no longer continue the research. My hope was to be able to have the tool validated and used as an reliable instrument for physical therapists and sports psychologists to recognize the early onset of situational depression for injured athletes. I believe that this IAQ would be of great benefit to the sports medicine community, so I am hoping to have it validated in the near future.

There is a great need for sports psychologists to be on staff or nearby in order to create a comprehensive clinic for sports medicine practices. Sports psychology consultants can assist athletes with the mental strategies needed to overcome injury and return to play. Additionally, they can assist athletes with situational depression at its onset instead of waiting until the patient feels lost. Sports psychology consultants assist athletes to not only in perform better but to cope with injury, eliminate anxiety, and learn mental strategies to overcome specific obstacles. Sometimes athletes need to see a sports psychologist or consultant. These psychological practitioners are best equipped to spearhead the healing process of the psyche. Not only would athletes have a better chance of adhering to their rehabilitation programs, but their exposure to mental strategies and systematic goals in the process of recovery would likely help them far beyond their recovery from injury, especially if the injury is career ending.

CHAPTER SEVEN

A COMPREHENSIVE PLATFORM TO IMPACT THE PSYCHES OF ALL ATHLETES

Through failure or loss, there is always room to grow, become better, and perhaps achieve more success than playing your sport could have ever given to you.

What is your exit strategy? How do you cope when the cheering stops? Charli Turner Thorne, the women's basketball coach at Arizona State University, has formed a comprehensive mental health team to assist her athletes. Thorne understands that your mind and body need to work together to perform to the best of your ability in a sport. The tools that her athletes receive will carry them further than just on the court. Athletes are tough on themselves, especially when they are injured or their careers end.

Why do athletes punish themselves? Why does it sometimes take them longer than others to overcome the loss of their careers? For them, there is always the question: "What do I do now?"

When you have staked a claim in your identity as an athlete, you set yourself up for loss. In hindsight, being able to channel the passion and thoughts of who you are as an athlete into who you are as a person is so much more fulfilling. Once you find that, always remember that you will be successful at anything you attempt.

BUILDING MENTAL STRENGTH

Developing positive mental strategies out of traumatic athletic events is multifaceted. In order for the injured athlete to perform successfully in rehabilitation, the athlete must believe they are going to be all right. Quite often, there is so much physical pain that it is difficult for the athlete to see how everything will be okay from an emotional stand-point. When an athlete goes down, so does their confidence. The most important thing an athlete can do is to build that confidence back up before rehabilitation. This can be done by discussing short-term goals and expectations while also facing the long-term realities of the injury.

I have asked many athletes if I could speak with them regarding the struggles they felt toward their respective sport. Unfortunately, speaking about what hurts the most is often very difficult and therefore many declined. Although it can be extremely cathartic, the athlete must decide for themselves to let go and talk about their pain in order to grow from it.

There are many books out there that discuss the transition out of sports. For most, it can be an easy transition, but for some (like myself), the transition is brutal. We have to remember that we all grow at different rates and can respond in different ways to similar situations. Losing an athletic career is no different. Athletes need to know that it is okay to hurt, but it's not okay to live in that pity pool. I know because I lived in it for a long time. I admit that at times when I have discussed my past athletic endeavors, I felt embarrassed that I never got to achieve what I thought would be success.

Lately, whenever I discuss my past, I am proud of what I achieved regardless of the outcome because I have come so far since losing my athletic career. Had I not suffered through what I thought was a failure, perhaps I wouldn't be where I am now. There is something to be said for loss. Although it may take decades to come to that realization, it is not about how fast you get through this journey. Instead, it is about where you end up and how you get there. Life is not a sprint.

TRANSITION AND EVOLVING YOUR PASSION AND LOVE OF YOUR SPORT

Sports psychologists and/or consultants should understand that the end of an athletic career can lead to a traumatic transition for the athlete. Realistic and positive goals must be set to create hope and avoid the situational depression that can become chronic. Athletes have an energy that needs to be channeled in a positive capacity for them to realize they still have limitless potential, even if it is not on a court or field. Some athletes will miss playing and the euphoria that comes with it, but success does not only have to come from a game.

Striving to be the best and knowing that you still have value even after your career is over can be an awakening for the injured psyche. Create a mantra, visualize it, speak it, and do it. Michael Phelps has found exercising and journaling his feelings to be helpful for him. I always tell my athletes to find a mantra for their competition. "I will not be broken" and "I will find the love that I want and have the life that I want" have been my personal mantras for the past few years. Throughout my bouts of depression, those mantras have helped me stay strong. The power of positive affirmations is contagious within your mind. If you tell yourself you cannot do something, then you won't. Instead, dominate your mind with positivity. You did it when you played your sport, so why not try this same tactic in all your future journeys? Feed your brain with positive reinforcement through social activity, exercise, and leisure activities—even the television shows you choose to watch. Just like you are what you eat, your brain will manifest what you feed it and that will be translated into thoughts.

The pain may never go away entirely, but you can still rebuild yourself. Never allow one door to close without busting down another. As an athlete, you would not have gotten as far as you have without pushing yourself to your limits; this time, you must set your goals higher, climb over that wall, and let your heart guide you through whatever comes your way in life.

When working with injured athletes, I tell them to set one goal at a time. Goal setting, as a motivational tool, allows athletes to translate commitment into specific and relevant actions.[18] Goal setting can empower an injured athlete as long as the goals are realistic and short-term. The acquisition of small successes, such as getting physically stronger, leads to becoming mentally stronger. However, this journey takes time.

Working with injured athletes takes patience. They need not only physical assistance but social and emotional support too. In order for the injured athlete to perform successfully in rehabilitation and in life thereafter, the athlete must believe things are going to be all right. This is where social support from the athlete's coaches, teammates, friends, family, and rehabilitation staff is imperative.

Perhaps the best approach to help athletes who have ended their careers is to practice the same things I learned through my grief counseling studies. The goal of grief counseling is to help a survivor find closure from a past event. The interesting part of this counseling is to increase the reality

---

18. S. Gordon, "Sport Psychology and the Injured Athlete: A Cognitive-Behavioral Approach to Injury Rehabilitation," *Sport Science Periodical on Research, Technology and Sport* 1 (1986): 1–9.

of the loss and to keep the memory of the past alive while reinventing oneself. Goal setting has been at the forefront of bereavement counseling. Support groups for athletes who have experienced the same issues will allow them to see that they are not alone in what they are experiencing. The game might have ended for them, but there can always be a new start. Maybe the path was meant to end just so a new life could arise. But how can someone who feels isolated in their dark thoughts find a new passion?

I believe in providing mental tools and suggestions for best practices for injured athletes. However, it is imperative that all counseling be based on theoretical frameworks of human behaviors and ideologies. It is easy to provide techniques, but it is more important for the psychologist to know the person they are working with fully, and not just their issues. This is relevant because all athletes are affected differently and for different reasons.

I have identified a few helpful techniques through my research and studies in athletic injury and the sense of loss. Keep a journal, write what you feel, set positive and realistic goals, propose mantras to self-talk, and influence positive outcomes within your inner self. Writing can help alleviate the pain of loss through the expression of deep, inner feelings that you may not want to share with anyone until you work through them on your own first.

The technique of writing mantras can be considered a form of cognitive restructuring. Mantras are positive self-affirmations that you can write down and place in various areas around the house as reminders for yourself. "I will not be broken" has helped me to remember that nothing can defeat me or my mind. It took a long time to get where I am psychologically, but the use of positive self-talk and mantras were at the forefront of my mental evolution.

Success is truly measured by a fulfilled heart. As fulfilling as it is to play a sport that you have worked so hard for and truly love, so is finding a new passion once your sport is over. Often, we are trying to reach the goal so badly that we miss the whole meaning behind why we were doing it in the first place. Sports give athletes success, but it is important to know that success can come from many different venues. When an athlete's sports career inevitably ends, they should have an idea of what comes next. When that darkness surrounding an uncertain future does hit you, the above-mentioned resources will be there to assist.

For those of you reading this book who are still playing or coaching, now is the time to think outside of the game. It may not seem like it, but there is so much more for you outside of playing your sport.

PUSHING FORWARD

As athletes and coaches, we often work from playbooks. This is something the injured athlete should recall when they are feeling lost. They can pull from their mental playbook and consider all of the mantras they have used over the years, the variety of techniques they used to overcome stress, and the adversity they met during competition to find their new path.

Athletes are more versatile than they may give themselves credit for when stricken with the abrupt end of a career. There are so many tools and techniques that they have used along the way to handle competition, and they need to realize that those same tools have been evolving within them to overcome this new impediment.

I wish I could say it is much like a rebirth, but it's not. It is actually a death of a part of yourself; you must choose to use all of the good parts that are still living deep within your soul. An embodiment of those strategies needs to surface.

All athletes face challenges within their careers. Within these challenges, coping skills and mental strength are generated. Although the athlete may not see it at the time, it is there. Personal goals are critical to regaining self-esteem and the motivation required to cross this new finish line. The finish line is placing the past behind you, thrusting forward, and finding out what else you were meant to do. The athletic journey was only a portion of your life. Believe it or not, that journey gave you critical life skills that will carry you further than you give them credit for in your dark times.

Many athletes who feel lost at the end of their careers feel useless in the "real" world. So, the posed question is: "How will I find what I love to do?" Just like the princess, sometimes you need to kiss a lot of frogs. What I mean is that you need to try out different things that you might have dreamed of doing when you were an athlete but never had the time to do.

One of the best recommendations I have as a sports psychology professional is for athletes to talk openly about the ends of their careers and their losses. First and foremost, speak about your emotions. There may not too many people who will understand, but ultimately it will be cathartic for you. It is okay to feel the myriad emotions that arise from such a loss. Find a support group and/or a psychologist to assist you with the journey of transition. Not all athletes can do it alone, and that is alright. You may feel alone in your circumstance, but you are not alone in what you are feeling. Know that there is no time frame for when you will feel free of the grief that comes about with this transition. For me, it has never gone away, but it has gotten better. As stated before, its much like the death of a loved one: you always miss them, and it hurts at certain moments, but it gets easier. Some athletes may ask, "So, what if the pain never goes away?" True, the sense of loss may never go away fully, but it will not be as fresh as it was when your world first came crashing down.

SOCIAL SUPPORT

One of the most important aspects in any type of transition, whether it be a retirement or a career-ending injury, is a social network. Social support is so important especially because the absence of it can be psychologically detrimental. When I was injured, I was lost. My family, friends, and team were all gone, and I felt isolated in my thoughts and feelings.

Social support can be defined as "An exchange of resources between at least two individuals perceived by the provider or the recipient to be intended to enhance the well-being of the recipient."[19] The support an athlete receives from family, teammates, friends, etc. can have a significant impact on the athlete's ability to cope. Athletic injury can be

---

19. S. S. Shumaker and A. Brownell, "Towards a Theory of Social Support Closing Conceptual Gaps," *Journal of Social Issues* 46 (1984): 11–36.

stressful, and social support can help to alleviate some of the pressure the athlete may be experiencing.[20] Unfortunately, there are instances when athletes do not receive the support they need and times when they do not recognize their need for support.

Athletes are disciplined and accustomed to having a set schedule. When they transition out of their sports, they frequently experience a sense of discontinuity or disconnect. They are not accustomed to the sudden changes in their athletic agenda. This results in feelings of separation and loneliness,[21] which can lead them to withdraw from contact with their teammates and loved ones. This is the exact opposite of what would help them.[22]

This is certainly what I experienced, as I did not know what to do or who to turn to and did not seek any support. The need to provide support to athletes in a transitional period has finally been recognized in the field of sports psychology but has not yet been recognized in all sports communities. Allen Watson and Bobby Hurley expressed the importance of the support system they found from their families. Hurley Jr. stated, "Luckily for me, I can thank my family, friends, and fans for the tremendous amount of social support they provided for me. Everyone had my back after the accident, including Coach K. People were very happy that I was alive.

---

20. D. Pargman, *Psychological Bases of Sport Injuries* (Morgantown, VA: Fitness Information Technology, Inc., 1999).

21. J. Crossman and J. Jamieson, "Differences in Perceptions of Seriousness and Disrupting Effects of Athletic Injury as Viewed by Athletes and Their Trainer," *Perceptual & Motor Skills* 61 (1985): 1131–4.

22. Shane Murphy, *Sport Psychology Interventions* (Human Kinetics, 1995).

Because of this support, I went back home to rehabilitate despite how difficult the process was." This system is pivotal at the onset to assist injured athletes in finding their way. It will also help them know that they have people behind them who care and will be by their side as they physically and emotionally recover.

When you are an athlete, you spend every minute with your teammates and coaches. So, when you become injured, you can't help but feel stuck in solitude while dealing with all the physical and psychological damages of your injury. You feel alone, as if no one can understand what you are going through. If you have a support team, they may realize your struggle and see your sadness even before you do. That's why social support is paramount for anyone who is suffering through an injury or any serious life transition. For me, living through it was tough, especially without having any family or friends who understood me nearby. I was almost twenty years old and everything I ever worked for had gone up in flames. My family was almost three thousand miles away. Instead of giving up, I made it my mission as a sports psychology consultant to work with athletes and help them with anxiety, transition out of sports and overcome their injuries.

Use the advice of others to help fuel your passions. It is okay to grieve but remember to use retrospection of past experiences to help you fill the void. This can create a better balance for your new take on life outside of sports. Samantha McKay discussed that it took her a while to find a balance between her personal and athletic lives, but she did eventually find that balance thanks to a sports psychologist at the University of Dayton.

There is not enough that can be said for social support. It empowers the athlete and helps them feel that someone has their back when they are going through tough times. Samantha no longer feels like she has to play for anyone else. She carries her supporters and the weight of her injured teammates with her no matter what, and this burden has been both beneficial and detrimental. Samantha states: "As athletes, we have our own motivations." She does play for herself, but she still plays for the fans too. She finally has been able to deal with the past and let it all go. It became unbearable when all the stress of her athletic life was translating into to her regular one.

WEIGHT OF GOLD DOCUMENTARY

Recently, I saw the trailer to *Weight of Gold*, an HBO documentary that discusses the mental and psychological trials that Olympic athletes suffer once the Olympics are over. This documentary (which I admittedly have not yet watched in full) looks at how athletes have everything at their disposal for physical performance but not for mental health. This documentary caught my attention because it finally shows athletes speaking up and being proactive about metal health. Since my injury, I have always hoped more athletes would spread the word of what athletes 'experience and how some may need help.

Often, I find, when speaking to athletes about injury and recovery, that there is a stigma to mental health assistance. Athletes feel that they are weak if they reach out for mental and psychological well-being assistance, so they choose to suffer through it.

Olympic athlete Michael Phelps supports this documentary and says that it could help other athletes dealing with mental health issues. Phelps himself struggled after the Olympics to the point that he contemplated suicide, so he sought assistance for his mental well-being. He has been interviewed many times saying, "It is okay to not be okay!" Phelps is saying that it is okay to struggle. It is normal to not feel okay about your psychological circumstances and the issues that weigh on your mind over the feeling of loss. However, there should be assistance for these athletes at the end of the Olympics to get them over the hump of the Olympic "high." They walk out of the Olympics on top of the world, and then it is over. I can only imagine that it must feel like stepping off of a cliff.

Athletes need a comprehensive model where sport and mental performance go hand in hand. Olympic athletes, like amateur and competitive athletes, are not isolated in their identities. Olympic athletes need to know their value and understand their worth beyond what type of product they can become sponsors for. Like other athletes, they need to be able to properly value themselves, but where are the tools for them to do that? Ultimately, there needs to be a platform designed to assist all athletes who are at the ends of their careers.

Athletes need a space for their voices to be heard. I always make the point that if the mental game is not up to speed, the physical game will fall behind too. If the athlete is not in the right space mentally, they can fall down a slippery slope of darkness. I have been there, and it can be scary.

Playing sports has always been a coping mechanism for me. When I am not participating in something athletic and/or active, I find that I am more anxious. In order for the mind-body connection to be maintained, there needs to be something fulfilling that can keep the mind occupied. As athletes, we get accustomed to a regimented lifestyle, and, when it ends abruptly, it disrupts that connection. Therefore, it is imperative that all athletes who are at the end of their careers find something that creates a calm mindset.

We all fear failure, but true success is a mindset, and from that mindset comes peace within our souls. Figure out what will truly make you happy and go for it. Do not just speak about it—put the time into researching and doing it. We only have one life to live, and constantly reflecting on what could have been will get you nowhere. It is okay not to be okay and to lay in your pity pool for a bit, but you eventually have to swim the hell out of it and go for the gold standard you see for yourself. In the end, no one can do it for you.

Transitioning from sport is not an easy task, and I can say from experience that it took me a long time. However, I was not prepared and did not have the supportive resources that are available today. I leave you with this: always know what drives you; seek out what you love and do it. Pure success is finding peace within your soul. All the gold medals and championships in the world cannot give you peace because your time in the spotlight will end. There is always another course to follow—you just have to believe.

Dr. Miele's Key Points:

1. An athlete never loses their motivation if properly directed and reminded that even though there was a loss, there still is so much to gain from past lessons

learned in their sport. There can always be a different or parallel dream that is just as or even more fulfilling than playing sports.

2. Identifying when athletes lose themselves will often be done by a coach, friend, or sports psychologist before the athletes know it themselves.

3. The mind will only be defeated if it fails to identify its strengths.

4. Sports performance needs to be comprehensive. Mental and physical training need to go hand in hand. You cannot have one without the other. The mind and body must be in sync.

5. The stigma of reaching out to take advantage of mental health professionals needs to be extinguished.

The most important takeaway from these stories is that athletes should now be wondering what fuels them. If you had the drive to play a sport, then you have the drive to be successful elsewhere. It is important to sit down and think about what you love to do. Whether it be drawing, writing, or medical work, the effort you once put into training for success as an athlete can be transitioned to any other activity. Personally, the pain from my loss of basketball and the wonderment of what could have been will always be there, but I have found satisfaction in my life knowing that I have helped hundreds of children sort out their dreams in life and athletics.

There are many warning signs for athletic trainers, coaches, parents, and other athletes to be aware of. If an athlete is showing critical signs of emotional distress, being able to identify them is paramount.

1. Changes in personality/mood
2. Sleeping longer than usual or sleeplessness
3. Changes in appetite
4. Isolation from family and friends
5. Easily agitated
6. Fatigue or lack of energy
7. Difficulty concentrating
8. Sadness
9. Felling worthless
10. Thoughts of suicide

Here are some resources if someone you know needs assistance.

Mental Health Awareness and Resources for Athletes in Need

- American Psychological Association Psychologist Locator: www.locator.apa.org

  The psychologist locator makes it easy for you to find practicing psychologists in your area. It allows you to consider many factors in searching for psychologists, including their areas of specialization, gender, insurance accepted, languages spoken, and much more.

- Society for Sport, Exercise & Performance Psychology: www.apadivisions.org/division-47. An accumulated set of resources for sports and psychology professionals.

- Mental Health Educational Resources: www.ncaa.org/sport-science-institute/mental-health-educational-resources

The NCAA Sport Science Institute is a leader in providing health and safety resources to college athletes, coaches, athletics administrators, and campus partners. The SSI provides educational resources for member schools to promote and support the health and well-being of student-athletes.

- Athlete Transition Services: www.atscorp.org

  Provides workshops for college and professional athletes to help prepare players for the transition out of sports.

- AspenPointe: www.aspenpointe.org

  A Colorado Springs-based behavioral health care provider. It also offers a 24/7 Walk-In Crisis Service at 115 S. Parkside Drive with no appointment necessary.

- American Foundation for Suicide Prevention: www.afsp.org

  Learn about suicide, how you can help prevent it, and resources for those affected.

- Hilinski's Hope: www.hilinskishope.org

  A nonprofit founded by Tyler Hilinksi's family to support programs that destigmatize mental illness in student athletes.

- Sidelined USA: www.sidelinedusa.org

  A nonprofit organization that helps athletes who were medically forced to retire find their next pursuit.

- Speedy Foundation: www.thespeedyfoundation.org

  A nonprofit organization whose mission is to prevent suicide, support mental health education, and promote conversations to end stigma.

- Talkspace: www.talkspace.com

  An online therapy tool for the general public that is also versed in specifically helping athletes.

- The Level Field Fund: www.levelfieldfund.org

  A community-supported organization that helps finance Olympic athletes while they compete.

- *The Transition Playbook for Athletes: How Elite Athletes Win After Sport*

  A book co-authored by former Dallas Cowboys center Phil Costa that documents more than 100 elite athletes' journeys with overcoming the transition out of sports.

- The US Center for SafeSport: www.uscenterforsafesport.org

  A Colorado-based nonprofit focused on ending forms of abuse in sports.

- https://www.umttr.org/about-us

  UMTTR was founded in Potomac Maryland to empower schools, youth athletic organizations, and many other "peer groups" with the funds, information, and tools they need to create a positive, compassionate culture where every person matters. They aim to place healthy habits for emotional well-being and caring support at the forefront of everyone's daily interactions.

- Team USA—Mental Health https://www.teamusa. org/mentalhealth

The US Olympic & Paralympic Committee is committed to promoting sustained well-being for Team USA athletes. More than ever, it is critical that we empower those who are in need to seek assistance, while proactively delivering mental health resources and services.

REFERENCES AND RESOURCES

Brewer, B. "Self-Identity and Specific Vulnerability to Depressed Mood." *Journal of Personality* 3, no. 61 (1993): 344–54.

Brewer, B., J. Van Raalte, and D. Linder. "Athletic Identity: Hercules' Muscles or Achilles' Heel?" *International Journal of Sport Psychology* 24 (1993): 237–54.

Brammer, L. M., and P. J. Abrego. "Intervention Strategies for Coping with Transitions." *The Counseling Psychologist* 9, no. 2 (1981): 19–36.

Chadiha, Jeffri. "Life After NFL a Struggle for Many." *ESPN*. May 31, 2012, accessed Dec 22, 2020. https://www.espn.com/nfl/story/_/id/7983790/life-nfl-struggle-many-former-players/.

Coakley, J. J. "Leaving Competitive Sport: Retirement or Rebirth?" *Quest* 35, no. 1 (1983): 1–11.

Cohen, D. B. *Out of the Blue: Depression and Human Nature.* New York: Norton and Company, 1994.

Crook, J., and S. Robertson. "Transitions Out of Elite Sport." *International Journal of Sport Psychology* 22 (1991): 115–21.

Crossman, J., and J. Jameison. "Differences in Perceptions of Seriousness and Disrupting Effects of Athletic Injury as Viewed by Athletes and Their Trainer." *Perceptual & Motor Skills* 61 (1985).

Ford, J., and S. Gordon. "Perspectives of Sport Physiotherapists on the Frequency and Significance of Psychological Factors in Professional Practice: Implications for Curriculum Design in Professional Training." *Australian Journal of Science and Medicine in Sport* 29 (1997): 34–40.

Fox 6 Now Milwaukee. "Former Packers' Linebacker George Koonce on Giving Back," *Fox 6 Milwaukee*. June 11, 2012, accessed Dec 22, 2020. https://www.fox6now.com/sports/former-packers-linebacker-george-koonce-on-giving-back/.

Gagne, R. M., L. J. Briggs, and W. W. Wager. *Principles of Instructional Design*. Fort Worth, TX: Harcourt Brace Jovanovich, 1992.

Gould, D. "Stress Sources Encountered When Rehabilitating from Season Ending Ski Injuries." *Sport Psychologist* 11 (1997): 361–78.

Gordon, S. "Sport Psychology and the Injured Athlete: A Cognitive-Behavioral Approach to Injury Rehabilitation." *Sport Science Periodical on Research, Technology and Sport* 1 (1986): 1–9.

Hamson-Utley, J. Jordan, Scott Martin, and Jason Walters. "Athletic Trainers' and Physical Therapists' Perceptions of the Effectiveness of Psychological Skills Within Sport Injury Rehabilitation Programs." *Journal of Athletic Training* 43, no. 3 (2008): 258–64.

Heil, J. *Psychology of Sport Injury*. Human Kinetics, 1993.

Ievleva, L., and T. Orlick. "Mental Links to Enhanced Healing: An Exploratory Study." *Sports Psychologist* 5 (1991): 25–40.

Kleiber, D., S. Greendorfer, E. Blinde, and D. Samdahl. "Quality of Exit from University Sports and Life Satisfaction in Early Adulthood." *Sociology of Sport Journal* 4 (1987): 28–36.

Kubler-Ross, Elizabeth. *On Death and Dying*. New York: McMillan, 1969.

Lerch, S. "The Adjustment of Athletes to Career Ending Injuries." *Arena* 8 (1984): 54–65.

Miele, Laura. "Vancouver Olympics 2010: How Can We Give Athletes an Edge on Injury Rehabilitation?" *Podium Sports Journal* (2010). Accessed Dec 22, 2020. https://www.podiumsportsjournal.com/2010/02/17/vancouver-olympics-2010-how-can-we-give-athletes-an-edge-on-injury-rehabilitation/

Murphy, S. *Sport Psychology Interventions*. Human Kinetics, 1995.

Oatley, K., and W. Bolton. "A Social Cognitive Theory of Depression in Reaction to Life Events." *Psychological Review* 92 (1985): 372–88.

Pargman, D. *Psychological Bases of Sport Injuries*. Morgantown, VA: Fitness Information Technology, Inc., 1999.

Pearson, R. E., and A. J. Petipas. "Transitions of Athletes: Developmental and Preventive Perspectives." *Journal of Counseling and Development* 69 (1990): 7–10.

Petrie, T. A. "The Moderating Effects of Social Support and the Playing Status on the Life Stress-Injury Relationship." *Journal of Applied Sport Psychology* 5, no. 1 (1993): 1–16.

Petrie, T. A., and S. Stoever. "The Incidence of Pathenogenic Weight Control Behaviors in Female College Gymnasts." In *Sport Psychology: Applications and Concepts*, edited by R. Cox. Boston: McGraw Hill, 2000.

Rosenstock, Sue. "Depression and the Sidelined Athlete," *Sidelined* (2018). Accessed Dec 22, 2020. https://www.sidelinedusa.org/sidelinedinterviews/.

Sachs, M. L., L. S. Tashman, and S. Razon. *Performance Excellent: Stories of Success from the Real World and Sport and Exercise Psychology.* Rowan and Littlefield: Lanham, 2020.

Sage, G. *Introduction to Motor Behavior: A Neuropsychological Approach.* 2nd ed. Reading, MA: Addison-Wesley, 1977.

Scutti, Susan. "Michael Phelps: 'I Am Extremely Thankful That I Did Not Take My Life.'" *CNN.* January 20, 2018, accessed Dec 22, 2020. https://www.cnn.com/2018/01/19/health/michael-phelps-depression/index.html/.

Shumaker, S. S., and A. Brownell. (1984). "Towards a Theory of Social Support Closing Conceptual Gaps." *Journal of Social Issues* 46 (1984): 11–36.

Udry, E., D. Gould, D. Bridges, and L. Beck. "Down but Not Out: Athletes' Responses to Season-Ending Injuries." *Journal of Sport and Exercise Psychology* 19 (1997): 229.

Vernachia, R., R. McGuire, and D. Cook. *Coaching Mental Excellence.* California: Warde Publishing. 1996.

Weibe, Shane. (2002). "More Than Just an Athlete." *Vaultworld* (2002) www.Vaultworld.com/articles.

Weiss-Bjornstal, D., A. Smith, S. Schaffer, and M. Morrey. "An Integrated Model of Response to Injury. Psychological and sociological Dynamics." *Journal of Applied Sport Psychology* 10 (1998): 66–9.

Werther, P., and T. Orlick. "Retirement Experiences of Successful Olympic Athletes." *International Journal of Sport Psychology* 17 (1986): 337–63.

APPENDIX

Injured Athlete Questionnaire (IAQ) (Miele, 2009)

Name: _____ Age: _____

Please circle one: Male / Female / Other What sport(s) do you play? _____ What did you injure?_____

_____

Does it require surgery, or have you had surgery already? Do you know how long will you be out of play? _____

Is this your first time in therapy/rehabilitation? If no, please describe other times and experiences _____

_____

How do you feel about your injury and the entire rehabilitation process? _____

Have you lost weight or gained weight recently? If yes, how much? _____

We are interested in knowing how you feel about your current injury and rehabilitation process. Please circle an answer for each of the following questions related to how you feel today. Do you:

	Never	Some Times	Most of the Time	Always
1. Feel hopeless?	1	2	3	4
2. Feel angry?	1	2	3	4
3. Feel tired?	1	2	3	4
4. Feel pain?	1	2	3	4
5. Feel happy?	1	2	3	4
6. Feel full of energy?	1	2	3	4
7. Believe you have failed?	1	2	3	4
8. Feel you have a good support system?	1	2	3	4
9. Believe you have good sleeping habits?	1	2	3	4
10. Feel isolated due to this injury?	1	2	3	4
11. Feel people understand your injury?	1	2	3	4
12. Feel your sport(s) is important to you?	1	2	3	4
13. Feel motivated to return to your sport?	1	2	3	4
14. Feel your injury is a major source of stress in your life?	1	2	3	4
15. Feel other areas of your life are suffering due to your injury?	1	2	3	4
16. Feel confident in your understanding of your injury?	1	2	3	4
17. Feel confident in your understanding of what will occur in therapy?	1	2	3	4
18. Feel confident in your entire rehabilitation process?	1	2	3	4
19. Believe physical therapy will help you in your recovery?	1	2	3	4
20. Believe that you will return to sports at the same level/performance?	1	2	3	4
Column Totals:				

IAQ Total: _____ / 80

ABOUT THE AUTHOR

Dr. Laura Miele is the owner of Mind over Body Athletics d/b/a Miele Forensic Consulting. She is an expert in fitness, sports, and recreation with specific expertise in sports psychology, personal training, fitness facilities management/operations, and injury prevention. She is an accomplished athlete as well as an experienced trainer, coach, and teacher.

Dr. Miele has worked with athletes on sports performance, transitions, anxiety, and sports injury. She presently is an adjunct professor at the University of Southern New Hampshire, Ohio University, and Montgomery County Community College. She gives presentations and runs clinics on subjects such as (but not limited to) mental toughness, anxiety, and team building.

With over twenty-five years of experience in various aspects of sports, fitness, and physical activity including the education, training, and supervision of athletes, she holds a bachelor's degree in Exercise Science and Physical Education, a Master of Arts degree in Education with emphasis in Administration, and a doctorate in Psychology with a specialization in Sport. She is a nationally certified and accredited interscholastic coach through the National Federation of State High Schools (NFHS). She is also a member of the Association for the Advancement of Applied Sport Psychology.

Dr. Miele played Division I basketball at Arizona State, played tight end for the Arizona Caliente of the Women's Professional Football League, and was also a New York Golden Gloves semifinalist in 2004. She began coaching athletes in 1986 and has been involved as a personal exercise and fitness trainer since 1994. Dr. Miele has traveled extensively throughout the United States and Europe as an athlete and coach and has been involved in consulting, coaching, and teaching a wide range of sports including basketball, gymnastics, volleyball, softball, baseball, football, archery, bowling, figure skating, hockey, boxing, wrestling, field sports, golf, soccer, swimming, track and field, gymnastics, tennis, and more.

Made in the USA
Columbia, SC
18 February 2021